THE INNER EYE OF LOVE

William Johnston was born in Belfast, Northern Ireland, in 1925, and was educated in Liverpool and at the National University of Ireland.

He joined the Jesuit order and then went to Japan in 1951, where he has lived ever since, receiving a doctorate in Mystical Theology from Sophia University, Tokyo, in 1968. He has made a special study of Buddhism and has taken an active part in the dialogue between Zen Buddhism and Christianity.

William Johnston is now Director of the Institute of Oriental Religions of Sophia University, and has lectured widely on East–West mysticism in Europe, the United States of America, Australia and Oceania. He has also been Visiting Professor at universities in San Francisco and Cleveland, Ohio.

Known as a translator from Japanese into English, William Johnston has written widely on East-West mysticism and contributed many articles to learned journals. He is the author of *The Mysticism of The Cloud of Unknowing*, *The Still Point : Reflections on Zen and Christian Mysticism*, *Christian Zen*, and *Silent Music*, the latter also available in Fount Paperbacks.

THE INNER EYE OF LOVE

MYSTICISM AND RELIGION

William Johnston

Collins
FOUNT PAPERBACKS

First published in Great Britain by
William Collins Sons & Co Ltd,
and in the USA by Harper & Row, Inc., in 1978
This edition first published by
Fount Paperbacks, London, in 1981

© William Johnston 1978

Made and printed in Great Britain by
William Collins Sons & Co Ltd, Glasgow

The Scripture quotations in this publication are from the
Revised Standard Version of the Bible, Copyright 1946,
1952 and ©1971, 1973, and are used by permission of the
National Council of the Churches of Christ in the U.S.A.
Quotations from *The Collected Works of St John of the Cross*
translated by Kieran Kavanaugh and Otilio Rodriguez,
Copyright ©1964 by the Washington Province of the
Discalced Carmelites, Inc, and used with their permission.
Paperback edition published by ICS Publications,
Washington, DC, USA. Quotations from *On Becoming A
Person* by Carl Rogers, Copyright ©1961, used by permis-
sion of Houghton Mifflin Company.

*FOR
MARY*

Contents

Preface

Recent years have witnessed an upsurge of interest in mysticism throughout the world. Psychologists and scientists begin to see that here is a phenomenon that cannot be overlooked in the study of the human mind. Religious thinkers like Henri Bergson, Martin Buber and Teilhard de Chardin look on mysticism as the very core of authentic religious experience. Orientalists see it as the key to the understanding of the religions of the East. And, most significant of all, thousands of ordinary men and women, feeling called to a deepening life of meditation and prayer, turn their attention towards mystical experience. All in all, mysticism is in the air we breathe; and it promises to be even more in the air of the new age into which we are moving.

And so I have written *The Inner Eye of Love*. The title, I believe, touches a chord in the great religions of East and West. All are aware that man born of woman is somehow in ignorance but that redemption is at hand. For he has a third eye, an inner eye, the eye of the heart, the eye of wisdom, the eye of love. When this inner eye is awakened man, blind from birth, sees the real glory and beauty and meaning of the universe. 'The eye is the lamp of your body. So if your eye is sound, your whole body will be full of light; but if your eye is not sound, your whole body will be full of darkness!' (Matthew 6:22,23). Surely these enigmatic words remind us that the important thing in human life is *to see*, to be full of light, not to walk in the dark.

In the opening chapters of this book I have attempted to sketch the background of this difficult word mysticism; and then I have given a preliminary description of mystical knowledge. It is possible that some of my readers who would ordinarily shrink from the word mysticism will recognize their own experience in this chapter. If so, let them not be afraid. Let them take courage and embark on the mystical journey which is described later in this book.

In the second section I turn to theology. One need be no great prophet to predict that Western theology of the next century will address itself primarily to dialogue with the great religions of the East. And I myself believe that this dialogue will be a miserable affair if the Western religions do not rethink their theology in the light of mystical experience. In this book I have highlighted the mysticism of Jesus as the key to the understanding of Christianity, just as the enlightenment of Shakamuni is the key to the under-standing of Buddhism.

I am aware that for many professional theologians mysticism is a peripheral affair – an esoteric and embarrassing subject which has rightly been relegated to an obscure position in the curriculum of any self-respecting school of theology. I myself have not been able to accept this point of view. And in this book I set myself the task of finding a place for mysticism in the overall discipline which we call theology. I followed the *method* of Bernard Lonergan and found myself drawn to the conclusion that mysticism is the very centre of religion and theology. I discovered that mysticism is the exquisitely beautiful queen before whom the other branches of theology bow down with awe and reverence like lowly handmaids. I also saw clearly that this queen is the Lady Wisdom for whom all religions search and in whose presence all religions meet.

The third part of my book is entitled 'Mystical Journey'. I hope that it will enlighten and reassure those men and women (and they are by no means few in numbers) who feel called to this joyful, if arduous, journey. Much of the material in these chapters comes out of lived experience – either my own or that of the many friends with whom I have talked and shared.

Needless to say, I had to deal with questions of nothingness and emptiness and darkness – all this negative terminology which fills the pages of mystics everywhere. And I came to the conclusion that mystical nothingness (and in particular the apparently negative *non-action*) is dynamite. It is the power that moves the universe and creates revolutions in human minds and hearts. For mystical nothing-ness, properly understood, paves the way for the dynamic action of grace. 'When I am weak, then I am strong,' cried Paul. And he never said a truer word.

The final section deals with action. Some theologians distinguish clearly, almost radically, between the mystical, passive religions of the East and the prophetic, active religions of the West. I have not been able to accept this dichotomy, as will be clear to the reader of my book. I have tried to say that mysticism, the core of all religious experience, has led to the most dynamic and revolutionary action the world has known. I believe that the great prophets were mystics in action – their inner eye was awakened so that they saw not only the glory of God but also the suffering, the injustice, the inequality, the sin of the world. This drove them into action and often led to their death. And just as the great prophets were mystics, so the great mystics had a prophetic role – even when this was fulfilled through a solitude and a silence and a self-oblation which spoke louder than words and shook the universe.

So many people helped me with this book that I feel it is not entirely my own. I cannot here mention the names of all; but I would like first of all to thank Juan and Rich and Dan with whom I live, who gave me constant support and encouragement ('How's the book going, Bill?') and with whom I discussed many of the problems treated here. Also Maureen O'Brien who helped me in innumerable ways; and Izumi Iwasaki who did the typing and editing. And finally there is my friend and colleague Edward Perez Valera who introduced me to the theology of Bernard Lonergan and kindly read my manuscript with eyes of love and compassion. To him and to many unnamed others I express my sincere thanks.

Institute of Oriental Religions,
Sophia University,
Tokyo,
1977

PART I

MYSTICISM

1. *Background (1)*

I

It is far from easy to define the word mysticism. Writing at the end of the last century William Ralph Inge cited no less than twenty-six different definitions of this word; and were he writing today he could cite fifty or a hundred. For he would find himself involved with Zen, challenged by Dr D. T. Suzuki, poring over books on yoga, contending with Thomas Merton, Mahatma Gandhi and the Maharishi Mahesh Yogi. Moreover he would have to deal with cosmic consciousness, with sudden illumination, with the occult and even with witchcraft. And he might well throw up agonized hands in despair.

I myself have decided not to do that. Faced with the burgeoning number of definitions and descriptions I will look briefly at the etymology of the word and then take my initial understanding of mysticism from the medieval Western tradition. Using this as a basis I shall try to remain open to modern thought and to the Orient. For while my language and way of speaking is taken from the Christian West I believe that the phenomenon towards which this language points is universal: mysticism is a profoundly human experience found in all cultures at all times.

In taking Western mysticism as my starting point I may seem narrow-minded and provincial in view of the great encounter of religions taking place before our eyes. Who is not aware of the treasures of mysticism in Islam, in Buddhism, in Hinduism, in Judaism, in all the great religions? But let me be frank. My first intention was to write a book on world mysticism or, at least, on Buddhist and Christian mysticism; but I found, not without anguish, that this was not possible.[1] Even if I had the erudition for such a project (and I have not), it would still be impossible to find a vocabulary or terminology that would cover all these religious systems. The longer I live in Tokyo the more I become aware of the enormous cultural gap which separates East and West. The way of

[1] I wrote the first sixty-five pages of such a book; and then, after consultation with two good friends, I threw the whole thing into the garbage can.

thinking, the words, the manner of expression of Buddhism and Christianity are so different that anyone who tries to write a theological book about both is doomed to superficiality and even to failure. For the fact is that Christians and Buddhists talk different theological languages.

Now I believe that a time will come, probably in the next century, when we or those who come after us will forge a common way of speaking and even some kind of common theology. But that is the future. At present I think it is only possible for a Christian to speak from a Christian standpoint and for a Buddhist to speak from a Buddhist viewpoint while we work towards mutual understanding, co-operation and love. Let us, then, write from our respective positions while opening our minds and hearts to the spirit in others. Let me write about Christianity as an insider and about Buddhism as a sympathetic outsider who has learnt very much and wishes to learn more.

II

Historically the word mysticism is associated with the mystery religions or mystery cults which flourished in the Greco-Roman world in the early centuries of the Christian era. Eleusinian, Dionysian and Orphic mysteries attained to great popularity, attracting thousands of spiritually hungry devotees to their esoteric rites and ceremonies. The mystic (*mustes*) was the initiate who in an oath of secrecy swore to be silent or, literally, to keep his mouth shut (*muein*) about the inner working of his new-found religion. In its original meaning, then, mysticism is associated with mystery and secrecy and the occult.

The word mysticism (like much of the terminology of the mysteries) passed into neoplatonism where it was associated with secrecy of another kind. Now it meant deliberately shutting the eyes to all external things, a practice which was central to neoplatonic meditation: one excluded the world in order to rise up to the One and to be 'alone with the alone'. The neoplatonists, Plotinus and Proclus, use the word *muo* of the closed eyes of one who is rapt in profound contemplation. While the eyes of the body were closed, the inner eye was open and was searching for wisdom.

The word *mystica* was introduced into Christianity by an anonymous Syrian monk, a Christian neoplatonist of the late fifth or early sixth century AD, who composed several theological treatises, one of which was named *Mystica Theologia*. To his works he quietly affixed the name of Dionysius the Areopagite who is mentioned in the Acts of the Apostles as a convert of St Paul; and the *Mystica Theologia* he fictitiously addressed to Paul's disciple Timothy.[1]

Though little appreciated at first, the works of the so-called Dionysius swept through the intellectual world of Europe after they were translated into Latin by the red-bearded Irishman, John Scotus Eriugena, in the ninth century. Initially some doubts were cast on their authenticity, but 'the pious fraud', as Aldous Huxley called it, turned out so successful that Albert, Aquinas, Bonaventure and the schoolmen greeted the author with the enthusiasm and reverence due to one who was close to St Paul and the New Testament. Commentaries on his works multiplied and even Dante sings the praises of the Areopagite. Only at the end of the nineteenth century was the identity, or lack of identity, of this anonymous monk definitively uncovered. He is now frequently called pseudo-Dionysius but I shall go along with his pious fraud and call him Dionysius.

While the prestige of Dionysius was greatly enhanced by his supposed proximity to St Paul, he was also highly rated because his writings were of value: he had a message: he had something to say. Moreover, he must have been deeply contemplative, and his *Mystica Theologia* was a real contribution to Christian thinking.

It opens with a passage which is important not only for the understanding of the thought of Dionysius himself but for the understanding of mysticism in other religions and cultures. For he describes how the mind ascends to the area of supraconceptuality and interior silence by transcending all images and thoughts, thus entering into darkness. The author, supposedly talking to Timothy, writes as follows:

Do thou, then, in the intent practice of mystic contemplation, leave behind the senses and the operations of the intellect, and all things that the senses or the intellect can perceive, and all things which are not and things which are, and strain upwards in unknowing, as far as may be, towards the union with Him Who is

[1] While Paul was at Athens 'some men joined him and believed, among them Dionysius the Areopagite and a woman named Damaris and others with them' (Acts of the Apostles 17:34). About this, the real Dionysius, little is known apart from this text. A tradition of doubtful historical value states that he was the first bishop of Athens.

above all things and knowledge. For by unceasing and absolute withdrawal from thyself and all things in purity, abandoning all and set free from all, thou shalt be borne up to the ray of divine darkness that surpasseth all being.   (*Mystica Theologia*, 1,1)

As can be seen, for Dionysius the word mysticism retains its meaning of secrecy; but now it is a secrecy of the mind which, possessing no clear-cut thoughts and images, remains in obscurity and darkness. A similar state of consciousness is found in Buddhism and in the mysticism of all the great religions, even when the theistic background of Dionysius is lacking. Plenty of Buddhist texts inveigh against concepts as deadly enemies of the great goal which is enlightenment.

For Dionysius, however, concepts are not deadly enemies. He accepts the validity of a theology of affirmation or, in Greek, *kataphatic theology*, whereby one uses concepts to affirm truths about God. But this knowledge is a poor thing and very imperfect compared with the knowledge which is found by denying concepts and going to God by unknowing – this is the theology of negation or *apophatic theology*. It is precisely here that one finds the most sublime knowledge. Moreover this knowledge, Dionysius maintains, is scripturally based; and he appeals to the example of Moses who climbs the mountain and enters into the cloud of darkness. Moses cannot see God – 'You cannot see my face; for man shall not see me and live' (Exodus 33:20) – but he knows God by unknowing; he knows God in darkness. He knows with the inner eye.

The insight of Dionysius is of the greatest importance for anyone who wishes to grasp the meaning of mysticism. For mysticism is non-discursive. It is not a question of thinking and reasoning and logic, but of transcending all thinking and entering into what modern people might call an altered state of consciousness. Here one is in darkness, in emptiness, in the cloud of unknowing precisely because one does not know through clear images and thoughts nor with the eyes of the body. There is a great inner silence, but it is a rich silence – and that is why we call it silent music. There is conceptual darkness; but the inner eye is filled with light.

III

The *Mystica Theologia* of Dionysius was translated into contemporary English by the anonymous author of *The Cloud of*

Unknowing in the fourteenth century.[1] It is interesting, however, to observe that the English translator made some small but significant additions to the text. Speaking of the mystical ascent into the realm of darkness that transcends thought, he says that one is drawn up *by love*. And in his translation of the passages about Moses ascending the mountain, he is careful to add that Moses was motivated and drawn on *by great love*. In making this simple textual change he is following a series of medieval commentators who had rendered Dionysius more totally Christian by centring his whole doctrine on love.[2]

So now the mind ascends to a realm of obscurity and darkness under the guidance of divine love. Love is the motivation and driving force behind the mystical journey – it is precisely love that leads one beyond thoughts and images and concepts into the world of silence. The inner eye is now the eye of love. If this seems difficult to understand, it may be helpful to reflect that human love often has the same effect. Profound human love may draw the lovers into a state of deep, unitive silence where thoughts and concepts become unnecessary and even superfluous yet where the inner eye, the eye of love, penetrates powerfully to the core of the other's being. Such human union is similar to (perhaps in certain cases it is identical with) the mystical loving silence about which the medievals write.

With this in mind it becomes possible to understand some of the classical definitions of mystical theology which were current in the Middle Ages and later in St John of the Cross:

1 Jean Gerson (1363–1429), Chancellor of the University of Paris: 'Mystical theology is experimental knowledge of God through the embrace of unitive love.'[3]

2 Bonaventure (1217–74): 'Mystical theology is the raising of the mind to God through the desire of love.'[4]

---

[1] The English title was *Denis Hid Divinity*. It is interesting to see that *mystica* is translated by the English word 'hid'. The medieval English translation was almost certainly made from the Latin and not from the original Greek.

[2] My readers will observe that the medievals were much less scrupulous about tampering with venerable manuscripts than our enlightened contemporaries. But do not judge them harshly. A different ethic prevailed at that time.

[3] *Theologia mystica est experimentalis cognitio habita de Deo per amoris unitivi complexum.*

[4] *Est animi extensio in Deum per amoris desiderium.*

3 St John of the Cross (1542–91): 'Contemplation is the mystical theology which theologians call secret wisdom which St Thomas says is communicated and infused into the soul through love. (*Dark Night*, 2:17,2).

4 Again St John of the Cross. Commenting on his own poem where he has written of 'a sweet and living knowledge' he writes: 'The sweet and living knowledge is mystical theology, that secret knowledge of God which spiritual persons call contemplation. This knowledge is very delightful because it is knowledge through love' (*Spiritual Canticle*, 27:5).

Similar definitions could be multiplied. But let me draw attention to three points.

First of all, it is clear from all the definitions that *mysticism is wisdom or knowledge that is found through love; it is loving knowledge.* This is a central point in my book.

Secondly, my reader will observe that Jean Gerson speaks of 'experimental' knowledge. This is important. For knowledge that is experimental is different from knowledge that is abstract. Experimental knowledge can be compared to feeling or touching; and experimental knowledge of God can only be obtained through love. This is the doctrine of the First Epistle of St John;[1] and it is the doctrine of the author of *The Cloud* who writes: 'For by love we may find him, feel him and hit him even in himself' (Johnston (2), p. 118). And again he says: 'Though we cannot know him we can love him. By love he may be touched and embraced, never by thought' (Johnston (1), ch. 6). Other medieval writers maintain that concepts can attain to God *as he is in creation*, but only love can attain to God *as he is in himself*.

Thirdly, it will be noticed that the definitions make no distinction between mystical theology and mystical experience, and that St John of the Cross identifies mystical theology with contemplation. These are points to which I shall return.

IV

In the thirteenth and fourteenth centuries, schools of mysticism flourished in the centres of spirituality and learning which arose within the great religious orders. There were Benedictine, Cistercian, Franciscan schools, as well as the so-called Victorines, a group of

[1] '. . . he who loves is born of God and knows God. He who does not love does not know God . . .' (1 John 4:7, 8).

theologians associated with the Abbey of Saint-Victor in Paris. Then there was the famous Rhineland Dominican school (and here the dark Dionysian influence was particularly strong though tempered by Thomist theology) with its big names like Eckhart, Tauler and Suso. There were Flemish mystics of whom the most famous is Jan Van Ruysbroeck. There was the cluster of English mystics, notably Julian of Norwich, Walter Hilton and the anonymous author of *The Cloud of Unknowing*.

While the voice of Dionysius influences this medieval mystical movement, the main inspiration comes from the Gospels, the Epistles of St Paul, the Psalms – the whole Bible. Particularly strong is the influence of the Fourth Gospel which Dean Inge calls the charter of Christian mysticism and of which he writes movingly: 'The Gospel of St John – the "spiritual gospel" as Clement calls it – is the charter of Christian mysticism . . . Perhaps, as Origen says, no one can fully understand it who has not, like its author, lain upon the breast of Jesus' (Inge, p. 45). In short, the Bible is the source of Christian mysticism as the sutras and the Hindu scriptures are the source of Buddhist and Hindu mysticism.

But there is also the influence of the Church fathers – of Augustine and Gregory and the rest. Then there is Bernard of Clairvaux (1090–1153), the last of the fathers, whose sermons on the *Song of Songs* were to have an impact on all subsequent mystical theology. Great, too, is the influence of Thomas Aquinas (1225–74) whose writings have exerted crucial influence not only on scholasticism but also on Catholic spirituality from the thirteenth century to our very day. And in the mysticism which flourished in this medieval period the whole emphasis is on love. This is a time which abounds in lyrical treatises on the grades of love, ecstatic love, the ladder of love; it is a time of discussions and controversy about disinterested love and the chaste and perfect love of God.[1]

In a theological framework, mystical experience was interpreted briefly as follows: God who is love infuses his gift of love into the soul. When man responds to this call he receives the Holy Spirit who is love personified. Writers of the time (including Thomas Aquinas) quote that text of the Fourth Gospel which says that love

---

[1] See, for example, *Of the Four Degrees of Passionate Charity* by Richard of St Victor in *Richard of St Victor: Selected Writings on Contemplation*, trans. by Clare Kirchberger (Faber and Faber, London). See also *The Mystical Theology of St Bernard* by Etienne Gilson (London, 1940).

calls down the Holy Spirit: 'If you love me you will keep my commandments. And I will pray the Father and he will give you another Counsellor to be with you for ever, even the Spirit of Truth . . .' (John 14:15,16). Mysticism, then, is based upon the indwelling of the Spirit and the 'divinization' of man. The Spirit who is love brings the gift of wisdom which is the special characteristic of the mystical life. But the mystic, possessing not only wisdom but other gifts as well, is described in the beautiful words of Isaiah:

> And the Spirit of the Lord shall rest upon him,
> the spirit of wisdom and understanding,
> the spirit of counsel and might,
> the spirit of knowledge and the fear of the Lord.
> And his delight shall be in the fear of the Lord.
> (Isaiah 11:2,3)

In this way the Spirit is the key to the understanding of mystical theology. The indwelling Spirit transforms us into the body of Christ and makes us cry out: 'Abba, Father!' (Romans 8:15). Or the same Spirit enlightens our inner eye and shows us the glory of the Son so that we cry out, 'Jesus is Lord!'

But let me say a special word about St John of the Cross, who lives much later but inherits the rich mystical tradition of the Middle Ages. He was a great poet; and for him mystical experience is a 'living flame of love'. This is how, in one of his beautiful lyrics, he describes the divine love which burns in his breast, paradoxically giving pain and joy, wounding and yet strengthening. And he sings ecstatically:

> O living flame of love
> That tenderly wounds my soul
> (*Living Flame*, Stanza I)

These words speak of his experience: they come straight from a wounded poetic heart. But when the mystic turns theologian and (at the request of his friends) interprets this experience in theological language, he states clearly: 'The flame of love . . . is the Holy Spirit' (*Living Flame*, 1:3). The flame is a person: divine love is personal; mysticism is a love affair and a romance. In centring his mystical theology on the indwelling Spirit and the theme of love, the Spanish Carmelite is in the full stream of traditional Christian mysticism which passes through Aquinas, the Victorines, Bernard of Clairvaux and the Church fathers to primitive Christianity.

It is precisely this burning love which is the core of the poetry, of the theology and of the life of the medieval, mystical movement. It is precisely this love which guides and points out the way when one is lost in the dark and groping for the light. For there comes a time in the mystical life when love is the only guide. All props have fallen away; all securities have collapsed; the mystic is naked and helpless; and only love is there to enlighten the way:

> With no other light or guide
> Than the one that burns in my heart
> *(Ascent,* Stanza 3)

Only love, only the Spirit, enlightens the darkness of the night.

2. Background (2)

I have pointed out that the word *mystica* entered the Christian vocabulary in the sixth century and became widely used only from the ninth century. Before that the word used for the phenomenon we now called mysticism was *contemplatio*. This also is a Latin word translating the Greek *theoria* which means 'looking at', 'gazing at', 'being aware of' and has a long history in the Greco-Roman world. Plato writes about the contemplative life which is a search for truth centred on philosophy or love of wisdom; and his disciple Aristotle, that seemingly cold Stagirite, becomes almost passionate and poetic when he writes of the pure joy of the contemplative life and the contemplative moment – that moment when man, exercising the divine element within him, becomes somehow like God and reaches the pinnacle of human activity.

Within Christianity the word was used by Augustine, Gregory, Bernard (mystics who had no influence from Dionysius) and it is still more commonly used than the word mysticism. Adolphe Tanquerey (1854–1932), whose work on Christian spirituality was once a textbook for students of theology, follows Thomas Aquinas in defining contemplation as 'a simple gaze on God and divine things proceeding from love and tending thereto' (Tanquerey, p. 649);[1] and he further quotes St Francis de Sales for whom contemplation is 'a loving, simple and permanent attentiveness of the mind to divine things'. As can readily be seen, these definitions resemble those of mysticism which I cited in the last chapter. Both contemplation and mysticism speak of the eye of love which is looking at, gazing at, aware of divine realities. In my book I shall henceforth use these two words interchangeably.

In early Christianity the word is associated with monasticism, with silence, with solitude, with a life devoted to the reading of sacred scripture, recitation of the Divine Office and the pursuit of wisdom. Clement of Alexandria, Origen and Augustine discuss the

[1] Tanquerey further quotes Thomas Aquinas: 'One delights in seeing the object loved. And the very delight in the object seen arouses a yet greater love.'

two lives: the life of contemplation symbolized by the quiet Mary Magdalen and the life of action symbolized by the bustling Martha. At first, Mary the repentant sinner who sits silently, lovingly and mystically at the feet of Jesus, is singled out as the model of Christian perfection while busy Martha is something of a second-class citizen. This tradition is found in *The Cloud of Unknowing* which makes an unfortunate distinction between those called to perfection (and these are the contemplatives) and those called to salvation – and these are the actives. But Thomas Aquinas, himself a Dominican friar, has more esteem for action as it appears in what he calls the mixed life. This is the overflow of mysticism: sharing the fruits of contemplation with others. For Thomas this is the more perfect life for two reasons. Firstly, because it is better for the candle to give light than just to burn, and in the same way it is better to share the fruit of contemplation than just to contemplate. Secondly, this mixed life was chosen by Jesus Christ – who taught and preached and healed and lived an active life.

For Thomas, then, the eye of love gazes not only on divine realities but also on human realities. Or, more correctly, it sees the divine in the human: it sees God in the world. Mysticism overflows into activity.

II

The turbulent years of the reformation gave birth to Ignatius of Loyola (1491–1556), the Spanish soldier saint who founded the Jesuits. And Ignatius, going beyond Thomas, envisioned a mystical life which would not only share with others the fruits of contemplation but would experience God in the hurly-burly of action. It was said that he loved not the desert but the mighty cities. Indeed, he challenged the notion that profound mystical experience could be found only in the silence of a monastic cell or in a hut in the desert. No. One could experience God deeply and joyfully in the anguishing contradictions, persecutions and humiliations which necessarily accompany an active life devoted to apostolate. And so he spoke constantly of the presence of God and of finding God in all things; and he opposed those of his companions who wanted to disappear into solitude for years in preparation for activity. He also talked constantly of the glory of God and of the greater glory of God. Surely this was because his inner eye was enlightened to behold that glory everywhere as well as the glory of the Risen Jesus. For he insisted that his order would be called the Society of Jesus – that and nothing else.

This mysticism of action, far from being a compromise, is extremely demanding. If one looks for a parallel in Eastern thought one will perhaps find it in *karma yoga*, the yoga of action which is splendidly exemplified in the life of Mahatma Gandhi. Here are some words of a Gandhi who experienced God in the midst of social, political and religious action, who saw God in his fellow-men. In his periodical *Harijan* he wrote:

> Man's ultimate aim is the realization of God, and all his activities, social, political, religious, have to be guided by the ultimate aim of the vision of God. The immediate service of all human beings becomes a necessary part of the endeavour simply because *the only way to find God is to see him in his creation and to be one with it.* This can only be done by service of all. I am a part and parcel of the whole and I cannot find him apart from the rest of humanity. My countrymen are my nearest neighbours. They have become so helpless, so inert that I must concentrate on serving them. *If I could persuade myself that I could find him in a Himalayan cave I would proceed there immediately. But I know that I cannot find him apart from humanity.* (Griffiths (I), p. 127)

Here is a true mystic in action, a true *karma yogi*. Gandhi seeks union with God through the world, union with God through mankind. This is different both from a humanism which seeks only man or from a world-denying flight that seeks only God. It is a discovery of the world's highest value.

But let me take another example from India, the sub-continent which constantly gives birth to religious genius. Mother Teresa of Calcutta relates a story about her sisters:

> 'During the mass,' I said, 'you saw that the priest touched the body of Christ with great love and tenderness. *When you touch the poor today, you too will be touching the body of Christ.* Give them that same love and tenderness.' When they returned several hours later, the new sister came up to me, her face shining with joy. 'I have been touching the body of Christ for three hours,' she said. I asked her what she had done. 'Just as we arrived, the sister brought in a man covered with maggots. He had been picked up

from a drain. I have been taking care of him, I have been touching
Christ. I knew it was him,' she said.   (Mother Teresa)

This is mysticism – and not a watered-down version either. It
conforms to all the definitions I have given in the last chapter:
it is supraconceptual knowledge through love. Moreover it is
experimental knowledge (remember that Jean Gerson insisted on
this) and contains nothing abstract. It is a profoundly incarnational
mysticism wherein the eye of love perceives Jesus in the broken
bodies of the destitute poor.

But let me return to Ignatius. The mysticism he envisioned was a
somewhat traditional interpretation of the Gospel and St Paul; but
it had never been formulated as a way of life for a group of people.
Consequently, the notion of a religious order which did not recite
office in choir and was always on the move created no small stir.

Yet mysticism in action developed within Christianity and is developing still. One of its great champions was Teilhard de Chardin
(1881–1955), himself a son of Ignatius. Passionately interested in
mysticism throughout his life, Teilhard had a deeply poetic vision
of a world vibrating with the presence of the cosmic Christ. He
believed that the mysticism of the future (and for him mysticism
really did have a future) was that in which the eye of love saw God
in the world and Christ Omega as the ultimate point of universal
convergence.

And so today we still find mystics sitting in the lotus in Himalayan
caves but we also find mystics demonstrating for justice in the
streets and suffering persecution in narrow prison cells. Moreover
we find mysticism in the lives of simple people who are constantly
moved by the Spirit.

III

But let me mention some salient features of this mysticism in
action.

First of all, it is not a question of blind fidelity to rules and
regulations but of following what Ignatius called 'the interior law of
charity and love which the Holy Spirit is accustomed to write and
imprint on the hearts of men'. And this interior law is a person: the
indwelling Spirit. It is a fact of experience that as the contemplative
life develops one finds oneself interiorly moved by the Spirit to do

this and not to do that. Indeed, the great art of mysticism in action is to discern the guidance of the Spirit: to be faithful to the voice of the Beloved who dwells within. 'If today you hear his voice harden not your hearts . . .' (Psalm 95). About this discernment I will speak later. Here only let me say that the Spirit does not ordinarily speak in clear-cut words and concepts but only through inspirations and movements which are dark and obscure like the supraconceptual knowledge of which Dionysius speaks – in this sense his communications are real mystical experiences.

I have spoken of Mahatma Gandhi as a fine example of contemplation in action. He did not speak precisely about the Holy Spirit, but he did talk constantly about the inner truth and the inner light to which he always strove to be faithful. 'Devotion to this Truth,' he wrote, 'is the sole reason for our existence. All our activities should be centred in Truth. Truth should be the very breath of our life. When once this stage in the pilgrim's progress is reached, all other rules of correct living will come without effort, and obedience to them will be instinctive . . . If we once learn how to apply this never-failing test of Truth, we will at once be able to find out what is worth doing, what is worth seeing, what is worth reading' (Duncan, p. 42). But it was only later in life that the movement of truth became a deeply-lived experience in Gandhi's life and he loved John Henry Newman's hymn: 'Lead, kindly light . . .'.

Now for a second characteristic of mysticism in action. In order to be attentive to the promptings of grace which are the voice of the Spirit one must cultivate what the old authors called purity of intention. This means that, liberated from enslavement to intellectual, emotional and spiritual self-interest, one seeks God alone. Here again one could quote liberally from Gandhi who on innumerable occasions spoke about that 'non-attachment' which he saw as the core of the *Bhagavad Gita*. We must act from love: never from desire of success or fear of failure. Nor must we be motivated by anger or hatred or vanity or ambition but only by love, by non-violence, by *ahimsa*.

A third characteristic of mysticism in action – and one which follows from the first two – is the loss of self. Gradually I must pass from an active life in which I am the centre to an active life in which Christ is the centre. This demands a real death; and Ignatius speaks of a life in which one acts constantly against one's ego: *agere contra*. His words here have been misunderstood. People have interpreted them as a form of self-torture or self-flagellation, as though one always had to do the unpleasant things; and it has often been said that Ignatius preferred ascetics to mystics. Yet this is not entirely true. His *agere contra* was not a rule to be blindly obeyed but was subject to the interior law of charity and love: it was, in short, a mystical grace leading to the loss of self: 'It is no longer I who live, but Christ who lives in me' (Galatians 2:20). One who loses self in this way constantly finds himself moving spontaneously and with great compassion towards the underprivileged, the poor, the sick and the imprisoned.

But what about solitude and silence in a life of active mysticism? Again we find Gandhi in his ashram maintaining one day of total silence each week – a day on which the great leader obstinately refused to speak a single word. As for Ignatius his attitude is not completely clear. On the one hand he himself spent long hours and months in solitude and silence. On the other hand he was wary of protracted periods of solitude and maintained that a person with the spirit of *agere contra* would achieve more in fifteen minutes than another in many hours. It seems to me that the time devoted to solitude will be governed by the basic rule: fidelity to the interior law of charity and love. There will be times when the Spirit drives a person into the desert as He drove Jesus into the desert to be tempted by the devil; and there will be other times when the same Spirit will drive the same person into the heart of action. Once again it is a question of discernment; once again it is a question of attentiveness to the voice of the beloved within.

IV

I have spoken about the movement to express mystical experience in scholastic categories which began in the thirteenth century and has continued until our very day.

At the beginning of this century we find a cluster of Catholic theologians who attempt to systematize mysticism, relying heavily on Thomas Aquinas and the Carmelite mystics, particularly St Teresa of Avila.[1] Though these theologians prefer the word contemplation they frequently speak of mysticism and call their discipline mystical theology. Their writings make some distinctions which are probably too tidy to suit the reality but which, never-

[1] Auguste Poulain (1836–1919); Adolphe Alfred Tanquerey (1854–1932); Reginald Garrigou-Lagrange (1877–1964); Joseph de Guibert (1887–1942), and others.

theless, are of some interest.

One such distinction was that between *acquired* and *infused* contemplation. Acquired contemplation, these theologians held, was not, strictly speaking, mysticism: it could be achieved by one's own effort aided by ordinary grace. Concretely it was a very simple kind of meditation in which one repeats a word or ejaculation again and again effortlessly and with great joy and unction. It was also called the prayer of simplicity or the prayer of simple regard or the prayer of the heart. It is not unlike the more developed forms of the Jesus prayer about which I shall speak later, except that not only the name Jesus but any religious word can be used. In its technique it resembles transcendental meditation where one quietly repeats a mantra or sacred sound; but unlike TM it is the expression of deep religious faith.

Infused contemplation, on the other hand, was equivalent to mysticism and was sometimes called mystical contemplation. It was the next step in the spiritual ascent, a step which could only be taken in answer to a special call. Its initial stages were characterized by a longing for solitude, an inability to think discursively, a profound inner silence and an obscure sense of presence. There were certain signs, very traditional in origin, by which the director or the person himself could judge that the time had come to enter into the void of this so-called infused contemplation or mysticism. About these signs I have written in some detail elsewhere and need not repeat myself here.　　　　　　　　　(Johnston (3), ch. 9, pp. 94–7)[1]

Yet another important distinction was made between the *concomitant phenomena* of mysticism and the *charismatic phenomena*. These latter were visions, revelations, trances, voices, ecstasies, psychic powers, telepathy, clairvoyance and the like: they were not essential and one must even be wary of them. On the other hand, the concomitant phenomena were inner peace and joy, love, the obscure sense of presence, the gifts of the Spirit. These, it was held, were always present in the experience.

Another interesting question discussed by these theologians was *the universal call to mysticism*. About this there were different

[1] It should be noted that some modern theologians, notably Karl Rahner, do not accept the distinction between the *ordinary grace* of acquired contemplation and the *special grace* of infused contemplation. They claim that all grace is 'special' being essentially of the same character: the self-communication of God. I have treated this elsewhere. See *The Still Point* by William Johnston ch. 8.

opinions. Some maintained that infused contemplation or mysticism was for an elite of specially chosen people. All Christians, they agreed, were called to perfection or holiness ('Be ye perfect as your heavenly Father is perfect' (Matthew 5:48)), but there were two paths to this goal – a mystical path for the few and an ethical path of solid virtue for the many. Theologians who held the latter view based their theory mainly on experience: they claimed that they met many deeply virtuous and pious people who had no trace of mysticism in their lives.

Others held that mysticism was a universal call. Put theologically, it was the ordinary development of the grace of baptism.[1] This theory is very traditional and has its roots in the Church fathers.

I myself believe in the universal call to contemplation, and I write this book in the belief that many of my readers are called to, or already enjoy, mystical experience. Yet in saying this I would like to recall some of the distinctions already made. First of all, while all may be called to the concomitant phenomena not all, obviously enough, are called to the charismatic. Again, mysticism may manifest itself in diverse ways according to temperament, education and culture. For this reason it may be difficult to discern the presence or absence of mysticism in a given person, and certainly it would be disastrous to force everyone into certain patterns like those of St Teresa of Avila or anyone else – there is an infinite variety of ways and mysticism may express itself in the most unusual and surprising manner. Again, while I believe that mysticism is a universal call, I would not be sure about when that call is made. To some it may come in early childhood, to others in adolescence or middle age, to others at the mysterious moment which we call death. But if mysticism is knowledge through love and if love is the great commandment, can we not say that mysticism is the core of authentic religious experience and that it is for everyone? And when I say for everyone I do not mean just for all Christians but for all men.

This is not mere theory. Later in this book I shall try to show that the most profound encounter of world religions takes place at the level of mysticism.

[1] Karl Rahner writes: 'Mysticism . . . occurs within the framework of normal graces and within the experience of faith. To this extent, those who insist that mystical experience is not specifically different from the ordinary life of grace (as such) are certainly right.' *Encyclopedia of Theology*, editor, Karl Rahner (Burns and Oates, London, 1975, p. 1010).

3. *Mystical Knowledge*

In order to understand the nature of mystical knowledge it is helpful to reflect on the human psyche as seen by some modern psychologists. With them we can picture the mind as a huge iceberg of which only the tip rises above the water, while underneath lies a whole world of wonder and terror, of light and of darkness, of good and of evil. Or we can see the psyche as composed of many layers of consciousness, one superimposed upon the other. Or we can reflect on the mind as a huge polyphony in which there are higher and lower voices. In our waking states ordinarily it is the higher voices that dominate and lead; but our conduct is all the time influenced by the lower voices too. In this way of thinking the word unconscious is, strictly speaking, a misnomer: nothing is unconscious in the psyche.

Whatever way we envisage it, the microcosm or inner universe is investigated by psychologists and explorers in consciousness from Jung to Aldous Huxley and from D. H. Lawrence to Timothy Leary. What precisely it contains we do not yet know but one thing is clear: the deep forces of the so-called unconscious are profoundly stirred by love. Love of man for woman or of woman for man, love of mother for child or of child for mother – this is the power that moves the inner universe and stirs mysterious, unknown, uncontrollable forces within us.

But there is a human question which psychology never asks and which leads people to religion; namely, what is at the deepest realm of the psyche? What is the basis or centre or root of all? Put in Jungian terms I might ask: When I go beyond the ego, beyond the personal unconscious, beyond the collective unconscious, beyond the archetypes, what do I find? And in answer to this all the great religions speak of a mystery which they call by various names: the Buddha nature, Brahman and Atman, the divine spark, the ground of being, the centre of the soul, the kingdom of God, the image of God and so on. They use different terms; but all, I believe, are pointing towards a single reality.

Coming now to mystical experience, we find ourselves confronted with the most powerful love of all – divine love, infinite love, unrestricted love; and this force shakes the so-called unconscious to its very foundation. The hidden layers of consciousness, normally dormant, are awakened; the inner eyes come to see; the inner voices begin to talk. But in particular it is the Holy Spirit who awakens within us; and it is to his voice that we must be attuned and attentive. Nor is this easy. We must learn the art of discernment in order to recognize his peaceful stirrings in the midst of the great chorus (sometimes a cacophonous chorus) which sings within. But about discernment I will speak later in this book. Here only let me stress the point that mystical knowledge arises from a deep level of the psyche which is ordinarily dormant. It is a different kind of knowledge from that which we ordinarily enjoy. Mysticism does not mean that we learn new things but that we learn to know in a new way.[1]

This same thing is expressed by the scholastics in a different psychological framework. For them all ordinary knowledge comes through the exterior senses, the windows of the soul, to the interior senses and then to the intellect. 'There is nothing in the intellect which was not previously in the senses' ran the old scholastic tag; but to this general principle mysticism was an exception. For mystical knowledge was not ordinary; it was directly infused into the soul bypassing, so to speak, the faculties. Technically they spoke of 'infused species' and said that God communicates himself 'by pure spirit' without any admixture of image or concept. Remember that I quoted St John of the Cross speaking of 'the secret wisdom which St Thomas says is communicated and infused into the soul through love' (*Dark Night*, 2:17,2). And elsewhere he beautifully describes this divine communication saying: 'In contemplation God teaches the soul very quietly and secretly, without its knowing how, without the sound of words, and *without the help of any bodily or spiritual faculty*, in silence and quietude, in darkness to all sensory

---

[1] St John of the Cross describes how mysticism leads one into what we would now call an altered state of consciousness: 'Besides its usual effects, this mystical wisdom will occasionally so engulf a person in its secret abyss that he will have the keen awareness of being brought into a place far removed from every creature. He will accordingly feel that he has been led into a remarkably deep and vast wilderness, unattainable by any human creature, into an immense unbounded desert, the more delightful, savorous and loving, the deeper, vaster, and more solitary it is' (*Dark Night* II, 17:6).

and natural things. Some spiritual persons call this contemplation knowing by unknowing' (*Spiritual Canticle* 39:12). Knowing by unknowing! Here St John of the Cross looks back to Dionysius. He means that one layer of the psyche knows and another does not know; or that one layer of the psyche (the sensory and intellectual) does not know what is happening at the other (the mystical). The left hand does not know what the right hand is doing. This is knowing by unknowing.

All this leads to the conclusion that mystical knowledge is totally different from the conceptual, imaginative knowledge that comes through the senses. It belongs to a different layer of consciousness; and for this reason it is ineffable and can never be described or adequately talked about. Again let me quote St John of the Cross: 'Not only does a man feel unwilling to give expression to this wisdom; but he finds no adequate means or similitude to signify so sublime and understanding and delicate a spiritual feeling. Even if the soul should desire to convey this experience in words and think up many similitudes, the wisdom would always remain secret and still to be expressed'. (*Dark Night*, 2:17,3)

II

To give a more adequate picture of mystical knowledge I would like to discuss some of its characteristics taking as my starting point the perceptive insights of the eminent psychologist William James (1842–1910).

His first characteristic I have already mentioned; namely, *ineffability*. James very simply and very wisely, attributes this ineffability to the fact that mystical states are more like states of feeling than states of intellect. 'No one can make clear to another who has never had a certain feeling, in what the quality or worth of it consists. One must have musical ears to know the value of a symphony; one must have been in love oneself to understand a lover's state of mind' (James, p. 371).

Indeed, mystical experience is ineffable because it is an affair not of the head but of the heart; and from time immemorial lovers remind us that the things of the heart defy all expression. The mystics love to quote those words of the Song of Songs:

I slept, but my heart was awake (Song of Songs 5:1)

Here the mystics, interpreting these words quite differently from the exegetes, declare that the mind is asleep, the mind is silent, reason and imagination and sense are quietly lulled to rest; but the heart is alert and awake. What conceptual language could express such loving awareness?

It was precisely because of the ineffability of the experience that the medievals welcomed the negative theology of Dionysius with its vocabulary of darkness, nothingness, emptiness and unknowing. Taken in the ordinary sense these words are negative and world-denying, but when applied to the deeper states of awareness they are profoundly meaningful.

William James's second characteristic is a *noetic quality*. By this he means that mystical experiences are not simply blind inner movements but have a definite cognitive content. 'They are states of insight and depths of truth unplumbed by the discursive intellect. They are illuminations, revelations, full of significance and importance, all inarticulate though they remain; and as a rule they carry with them a curious sense of authority for aftertime' (James, p. 371).

In other words mystical experience gives real knowledge. Yet, as I have pointed out, the cognitive content of mystical knowledge is non-conceptual and belongs to a different state of consciousness from that which we ordinarily enjoy. For this reason the greatest caution must be taken when one attempts to interpret mystical experience in conceptual language. Here great mystics have made pitiable mistakes. Let me quote from *The Cloud of Unknowing* a very powerful illumination which, the author claims, cannot be interpreted at all. The mystic is quietly and silently in the cloud of unknowing and then:

> Then perhaps he may touch you with a ray of his divine light which will pierce the cloud of unknowing between you and him. He will let you glimpse something of the ineffable secrets of his divine wisdom and your affection will seem on fire with his love. I am at a loss to say more, for the experience is beyond words. Even if I were able to say more I would not now. For I dare not try to describe God's grace with my crude and awkward tongue. In a word, even if I dared I would not.   (Johnston (1), ch. 26)

Here we are back to the ineffability of mysticism. Yes, it is cognitive;

it is true knowledge; but it cannot be adequately formulated in words.

The third characteristic of William James is *transiency*. 'Mystical states cannot be sustained for long. Except in rare instances, half an hour or at most an hour or two seems to be the limit beyond which they fade into the light of common day' (James, p. 372).

This is only partly true. The peak experiences are transient; but underneath is a permanent state, a deep peace which is compatible with joy or suffering, a sense of presence or a sense of absence, dryness or longing, boredom or monotony. All this is most undramatic; but it is truly mystical; it is the work of love in those deeper layers of consciousness. Indeed, it is the ground and basis of the transient, ecstatic moments.

For mystical experience extends over a whole life. As the author of *The Cloud* says, it goes to bed with you at night and it gets up with you in the morning. It is a permanent awareness which can exist in a very busy and active life.

The fourth characteristic is *passivity* – 'the mystic feels as if his own will were in abeyance, and indeed sometimes as if he were grasped and held by a superior power' (James, p. 372).

This again is true in that the mystics will say that they are moved by a power which is deeper than themselves. And yet this word 'passivity' must be used with the greatest caution. For while it is true that one layer of consciousness is passive and empty and dark, it is also true that a very powerful activity is going on at a deeper layer of the psyche. This is an activity which may continue for nights and days without fatigue to mind or body.

I consider the active dimension of mysticism very important and am wary of the word 'passive'. This is because there have been in all religious traditions schools of so-called quietism, and their voice can still be heard today: 'Be absolutely still! Empty your mind! Erase all thoughts from your consciousness! Blot out everything! Stop thinking! And this is mysticism.'

But this is not mysticism, oriental or occidental. This is nonsense.

III

The mystics of the Dionysian tradition speak frequently about the 'secrecy' of mysticism – mystical knowledge is 'hidden' in the depths of one's being. This is quite understandable in view of the fact that it belongs to a layer of consciousness which is hidden from, and inaccessible to, the intellect and the sensible faculties. 'Ordinarily,' writes St John of the Cross, 'this contemplation *which is secret and hidden from the very one who receives it*, imparts to the soul an inclination to remain alone and in quietude' (*Dark Night*, 1:9,6).

Secret from the one who receives it! How strange and how different from the popular conception of the mystical trip! So often mysticism is associated with lights and bells and incense and ecstasy; whereas ecstasy, pertaining as it does to the realm of sense, is a sign of superficiality. The deepest mysticism is more like the still small voice which spoke to Elijah. Yes, mysticism is secret from the person who receives it. And it is interesting to reflect that in Buddhism also the most enlightened person is often the one who does not know that he is enlightened: his enlightenment is hidden even from himself.

Now this point is very important and very practical. Not infrequently one meets people who have spent years in dryness, in inner suffering, in darkness. Their meditation is sleepy and uncomfortable and seems like a waste of time: they think they are doing nothing. But the tiny flame of love is burning quietly in the depths of their being; the loving knowledge is there in secret; their experience is profoundly mystical. This will seem less strange if we reflect that human love is often just the same. It grows secretly at night when no one is watching like the seed scattered upon the ground. Then one morning we wake up – and there it is! Quite often it is only in moments of separation and death that we advert to the depth of our own love. Or again human love may at first be filled with rapturous joy; but the lean and fallow years have to come.

And in the same way mystical experience may at first be delightful and filled with froth and joy; but eventually the call comes to go deeper and (wonder of wonders!) this going deeper in all the great mystical traditions is *a passage to the ordinary*. Remember how Zen keeps speaking of 'your ordinary everyday mind'. No longer the first exciting silence of discovery but an almost boring silence of penetration and familiarity, a 'becoming at home' as the author of *The*

Cloud would say. And I wonder if it does not take yet another enlightenment from the Spirit to recognize this seemingly hum-
drum experience as a real God-experience and to be faithful to the
time of the fallow ground (which may mean years of perseverance)
until the right time, the *kairos*, arrives.

But instead of patiently waiting, some modern people join in the
frenetic search for new experiences, for oriental meditation of all
kinds, for the soul-stirring illumination that will revolutionize their
lives. If they only knew that they are leaving the fruit to go back to
the rind! No one in their right mind would do this; but the problem
is that *the fruit is not recognized as fruit:* it is secret: it is hidden. That
is why discernment is so important; that is why it is so necessary that
contemplatives should meet someone who can understand their
experience or, at least, read some book with which they can resonate.
Otherwise they may not know what is happening in their lives and
may become discouraged.

But if they persevere, they come to love the darkness and the dryness; they come to see its beauty; or they come to recognize that the
darkness is no longer dark and the dryness is no longer dry. They
come to see that mystical knowledge is, so to speak, an acquired
taste. At first one does not like it at all; one recoils from a bitterness
which is so distasteful to the palate. Yet in time it becomes so sweet
and delicious that one would not exchange it for all the world. Again
St John of the Cross: 'If in the beginning the soul does not experience this spiritual savour and delight, but dryness and distaste,
it is because of the novelty involved in this exchange. Since its palate
is accustomed to these other sensory tastes, the soul still sets its
eyes on them. And since, also, its spiritual palate is neither purged
nor accommodated for so subtle a taste, it is unable to experience
the spiritual savour and good until gradually prepared . . .' (*Dark
Night*, 1:9,4).

In short, mysticism opens up a new layer of psychic life which is
bitter and unpleasant because of its unfamiliarity. But when the eye
of love becomes accustomed to the dark, it perceives that the darkness is light and the void is plenitude.

IV

Finally, let me say that many of those endowed with profound
mystical knowledge are very active people: the inner light has driven
them into the mighty cities and the maelstrom of a whirling world.

In such cases 'the obscure sense of presence' of which the mystics speak may become dynamic. I become conscious not only of the Spirit *present in me* but of the Spirit *working in me*, not only of Christ being in me but of Christ dynamically alive in me and driving me to union with his members and with the cosmos.

Such active people, it is true, need periods of silence and of solitude; but it is also true that they carry around in their hearts a great solitude which is also a great love – and this solitude continues in the midst of activity. Indeed, it is a solitude which is deepened by the hurt, the criticism, the disappointment, the betrayal, the human friction, the humiliation and the ordinary pain of living. Just as the beating with the stick or *kyosaku* deepens the Zen experience, so the ordinary contradictions of life (with much less pomp and ritual and solemnity) deepen contemplative experience. Indeed, without this kind of suffering it is difficult to see how one can die to self in order to live to one who rose from the dead. Frequently it is through the suffering of action that the inner eye is opened and we truly come to see.

PART II

MYSTICISM AND THEOLOGY

4. *Mystical Theology*

I

From what has been said it will be clear that there is a distinction between mysticism and mystical theology. Mysticism is the experience: mystical theology is reflection on this experience.[1] The medievals did not make this distinction clearly, as can be seen from my earlier quotations in which they identify mystical theology with mystical experience and call contemplation mystical theology. But the distinction is completely necessary today if we are to build up a theology that will speak to contemporary men and women and promote dialogue between the world's great religions at the level of mysticism.

I am aware that some people will maintain that only experience matters and that mystical theology with its theory and words and concepts is a useless accretion. While I would agree that mystical experience is the basic thing, that it is ineffable and that all efforts to formulate it are totally inadequate, I cannot accept the anti-intellectualism which would reject all reflection. No. We need to interpret mystical experience and to find its meaning. We need to distinguish the authentic from the inauthentic. Then there is the practical need to guide people, to protect them from mistakes, from illness, from illusion – to help them understand what is happening in their lives and save them from unnecessary suffering. Besides, must we not learn all we can, even conceptually, about the action of the divine in the human?

In the East we find something akin to mystical theology in the great religious philosophers and thinkers like Sankara and Nagarjuna. We also find numerous commentaries on Buddhist sutras and Hindu scriptures – for every religion has its holy books which are the source of its mysticism. But the practical aspects are incarnate in the living master or teacher. Here is a man who guides and who has the practical knowledge to do so. He knows what he wants; he

---

[1] Theology was traditionally defined as 'the science of God'. More recently, however, Bernard Lonergan defines it as 'reflection on religion'. Following this I understand mystical theology as reflection on mystical experience. See Lonergan (1), p. 267.

knows the nature of the experience towards which he leads; he is quick to detect error. The Oriental master has a fund of conceptual knowledge culled from his own enlightenment, from the enlightenment of others and from his assiduous reading of his own scriptures.

In the West also a great deal of practical knowledge was handed down orally, particularly in the great religious orders. At the basis of this is the Bible, particularly the Gospel, St Paul and the Psalms. But a science of mystical theology also evolved, a science which still exists but is in drastic need of updating. For every age must have its own mystical theology; and we need something new in view of the peculiar problems which confront us today. As Bernard Lonergan says in a slightly different context: 'There are real problems of communication in the twentieth century, and they are not solved by preaching to ancient Antioch, Corinth or Rome' (Lonergan (1), p. 140); and in the same way there are real problems of mysticism in the the twentieth century and we will not solve difficulties about the drug culture and oriental mysticism just by quoting Augustine and St John of the Cross. Assuredly the works of these mystics are of inestimable value and I quote them abundantly; but we must advance, and we must do for our generation what they did for theirs, remembering that we are children of an age which has made outstanding advances in psychology, neurophysiology, brain research and all aspects of inner space – to say nothing of biblical research, archaeology and ancient history.

If we wish to construct a modern mystical theology, however, there will have to be a much greater division of labour than in the past. Some people will reflect on mysticism from the aspects of psychology and medicine while others, working and collaborating with them, will devote themselves to the strictly religious aspects. It is about these latter aspects that I myself will speak.

II

If mystical theology is a science it must have data. Such data will be found in the experience of mystics living and dead, in the experience of mystics past and present, in the experience of mystics East and West. All the great religions already have their mystical theology, even though they may not use this term. They reflect on the seers and prophets of the *Upanishads* or upon the experience of great Buddhist mystics like the Zen masters Dogen and Hakuin. Even further there is reflection (and this is basic) on the experience of the Buddha himself when he found enlightenment sitting cross-legged beneath the Bodhi tree at Bodh Gaya. As everyone knows, Buddhism aims at nothing less than a repetition of this enlightenment of the Buddha: if I am a Buddhist, my aim is to re-enact within myself the experience of Sakyamuni and to become a Buddha.

Coming to a specifically Christian mystical theology, we must again ask about the data and the sources. Many books written on this subject have expounded the doctrine of the Rhineland mystics, the Spanish Carmelites, the medieval English mystics, the fathers of the Church – and we have the diaries of holy people and biographies of saints. Undoubtedly all this is of great value; but I would like to point out that the source of all Christian mysticism is – and must be – the Bible and in particular the Gospel. This is because the Christian mystical tradition states clearly that the aim of the Christian life is to become 'another Christ' (*Christianus alter Christus*) and in the process of becoming another Christ the Gospel is obviously the central inspiration. If, then, there is to be an updating of Christian mystical theology the first step is a return to the Gospel.

In saying this, however, I am immediately faced with a formidable objection. There are scholars who hold that the Bible contains no mysticism whatever: that mysticism is basically an oriental and non-Christian trend. This way of thinking stems from their understanding of the word mysticism (remembering I spoke of fifty or a hundred different definitions) which they associate with a monism or pantheism that is incompatible with belief in a personal God. At the risk of making a brief digression I would like to consider their viewpoint, simply selecting one scholar who seems to be representative.

The well-known scholar Friedrich Heiler distinguishes between prophetic or biblical religion and mysticism. This latter he defines as: 'that form of intercourse with God in which the world and self are absolutely denied, in which human personality is dissolved, disappears and is absorbed in the infinite unity of the Godhead' (Heiler, p. 136). Obviously if the world and self are denied and human personality is dissolved there is not much mysticism in the Bible or in any theistic religion which speaks of a relationship between man and God. But how valid is this definition?

No doubt Heiler understands mysticism in this way because of the phenomenon of 'undifferentiated consciousness' which is so central to oriental thinking and is found also in many Western mystics. This is the consciousness of one who transcends subject and object to enter into a state of pure oneness. Bede Griffiths describes it well:

> There is an experience of being in pure consciousness which gives lasting peace to the soul. It is an experience of the Ground or Depth of being in the Centre of the soul, an awareness of the mystery of being beyond sense and thought, which gives a sense of fulfilment, of finality, of absolute truth . . . It is an experience of the undifferentiated ground of being, the abyss of being beyond thought, the One without a second.   (Griffiths (2), p. 137)

Bede Griffiths is writing from the Indian scene but, as I have said, a similar form of pure consciousness is found in some Western mystics, and something analogous exists throughout East Asian culture where one hears of the non-self or no-mind condition called in Japanese *muga* or *mushin*. This state of consciousness is found in an intense form in the sudden illumination or *satori* of Zen. But I believe that it admits of degrees and is found in a simpler form in the Sino-Japanese arts such as the flower arrangement, archery and the tea ceremony. Here one identifies with the object (I *become* the flower or the bow) and one loses self. The experts tell us, however, that to attain to this state of consciousness takes years of discipline and training.[1]

Confronted with this consciousness in its various forms, Western philosophers (who feel happier when they can put labels on things and apparently control them) have freely used words like pantheism and monism, applying Hellenistic words to Oriental experiences. And a few scholars have made this oneness the kernel of all mysticism and the supreme achievement of the human mind.

But surely it is gratuitous to limit mysticism to this kind of thing. And surely it is equally gratuitous to decide that this is the 'highest' or supreme experience. It is true, of course, that all mysticism leads to oneness or unity; but there is a union of love in which far from losing my personality I become my true self, hear myself called by name and cry out: 'Abba, Father!'. This is the experience in which I

---

[1] This consciousness is frequently called the *non-discriminating consciousness* because no distinction is made between subject and object and there is no reasoning or thinking or conceptualization in the mind.

become the other while remaining myself. Or, more correctly, I become the other and become myself. Paradoxical, you will say. Yes. Mysticism is full of paradox.

And one more important point. This undifferentiated consciousness can only be labelled pantheism or monism if the subject passes from the psychological inner experience to the outer world, affirming that in the objective order the self and the world do not exist. And I am not at all convinced that many mystics have done this. They were more subtle than that – and scholars are still divided in their interpretation of the most radical monists like Sankara.

As for the Western mystics, they wrestled with this problem, for they experienced both the unity of all things and the fatherhood of God. But they were greatly handicapped by the Hellenistic psychology in which they were educated. This psychology speaks of intellect and will, or of memory, understanding and will – it speaks of the senses and the spiritual faculties. With such a psychology it is not easy to reconcile the unity and diversity of being.

In a modern psychology, however, which speaks of states of consciousness the problem is more easily solved. For here we can recognize a consciousness which sees unity (and such a consciousness undoubtedly exists) and a consciousness which sees diversity. These states of consciousness can exist at different times in the same person. Or (and this is significant) they can exist concomitantly in the same person in such wise that one sees unity and diversity simultaneously. I have written about this in *Silent Music* and need not repeat myself here (Johnston (3), ch. 7).

This has been something of a digression; but I think it was necessary because the notion that mysticism is 'pantheistic' or 'monistic' and in consequence non-biblical is widespread. Let me now return to the Bible.

First of all there, is prophetic experience. The scripture scholar John L. McKenzie, after discussing the various theories about the nature of prophecy, comes to the conclusion that 'the prophetical experience is . . . a mystical immediate experience of the reality and presence of God'. Indeed, he compares it with that of the great Spanish mystics:

The only satisfactory parallel to the prophetic experience is the phenomena of mysticism as described by writers like Teresa of

Avila, John of the Cross and others. They affirm that the immediate experience of God is ineffable; like the prophets, they must employ imagery and symbolism to describe it, with explicit warnings that these are used. They describe it as a transforming experience which moves one to speech and action beyond one's expected capacities. It grants them profound insight not only into divine reality but into the human scene. Thus the prophetic experience is such a mystical immediate experience of the reality and presence of God.   (McKenzie, p. 697)[1]

If we accept this thesis we can see the most profound mysticism in that chapter of Exodus where Moses hears his name called: 'Moses, Moses!' and is overwhelmed by the presence of God and the sense of the holy. 'Do not come near; put off your shoes from your feet, for the place on which you are standing is holy ground' (Exodus 3:5). Or again in Jeremiah: 'Before I formed you in the womb I knew you' (Jeremiah 1:5). Here also the prophet hears the inner voice and is liberated from fear (and this, be it noted, is a common characteristic of mystical experience): 'Be not afraid of them, for I am with you to deliver you, says the Lord' (Jeremiah 1:8).

In these experiences we find union with God, the sense of being loved, of being chosen, of being sent; and we also find a profound sense of personal uniqueness and unworthiness. I am a person loved by God, but yet I am far distant from him, unworthy to stand in his presence. 'And Moses hid his face, for he was afraid to look at God' (Exodus 3:6).

---

[1] Some theologians, notably, A. Ritschl, N. Söderblom, E. Brunner, and K. Kraemer, distinguish between Oriental mystical religion and biblical prophetic religion, claiming that these two types are mutually exclusive and irreconcilable. In an excellent article in *Concilium* (123, 1977) Peter Nemeshegyi shows that these two types are not incompatible but complementary. I myself maintain that mysticism, as I have understood it, is the core and climax of all religious experience and that it expresses itself sometimes in a life of solitude and at other times in a prophetic life of powerful activity. Karl Rahner writes: 'the prophetic element can (it does not have to) be connected with mystical experience' (*Encyclopedia of Theology*, edited by Karl Rahner, Burns and Oates, London 1975, p. 1010). St John of the Cross takes it for granted that the great prophets had mystical experience and constantly appeals to their example.

III

Keeping in mind that mysticism is the supraconceptual wisdom that comes from love we can find such experience throughout the pages of the New Testament. In particular we find it in the great contemplative prayer taught by Jesus: 'Our Father'.

'Mysticism in the Lord's prayer?' you will say. 'How simple can you get?' Yes. But the greatest Christian mystics have written commentaries precisely on the 'Our Father'. Origen, Cyprian, Teresa of Avila have found in its simple phrases treasures of mystical experience.[1] Thérèse of Lisieux, great contemplative that she was, sat quietly in the chapel reciting the 'Our Father', her heart sometimes filled with dryness and inner suffering. Yes. It is all very simple; but remember I said that mysticism is a journey towards the ordinary; remember that I quoted Zen about your ordinary everyday mind. Christian mysticism reaches its peak when, as another Christ in utter simplicity and trust, I allow the words of Jesus to well up from the depth of my being and cry out: 'Abba, Father!'.

And there is mysticism in the Sermon on the Mount. This is the mysticism of the present moment – a moment that is lived without anxiety about the future or fear about the past, without preoccupation about what I shall eat or drink. My Heavenly Father knows what I need before I ask. The Sermon on the Mount has (and very justly I believe) been compared to Zen in that it describes the undifferentiated consciousness of one who lives in the here-and-now with joy and without care: 'Therefore do not be anxious about tomorrow . . .' (Matthew 6:34).

One could go on to speak about the parables and the various aphorisms or *logia* of the Gospel of St Matthew – for these indeed strike a chord in the Buddhist heart. Or one could speak about the opening of the eyes of the blind (what a great enlightenment!) and how the inner eyes came to see the glory of God: 'But blessed are your eyes, for they see . . .' (Matthew 13:16). But let me say a word about *Jesus the mystic*.

Again, if mysticism is the wisdom which comes from divine love, can we not see Jesus as the mystic *par excellence*? Because love for

---

[1] Many of the Church fathers commented on the 'Our Father': Tertullian: *De Oratione*; Cyprian: *De Dominica Oratione*; Origen: *Perieuches;* Gregory of Nyssa: *Five Homilies on The Our Father;* Ambrose: *De Sacramentis*, lib v; Peter Chrysologus, *Sermones* 67–72.

his Father was the dominating passion of his life: 'Abba, Father!'. And the whole Gospel relates the drama of how Jesus loved the Father, how he was loved by the Father and how he offered himself for the world, praying for his disciples 'that the love with which thou has loved me may be in them, and I in them' (John 17:26).

Jesus, we can presume, being truly human grew in the knowledge of his divine sonship and in the realization of who he was. And one of his great mystical experiences takes place at the time of his baptism:

> And when he came up out of the waters, immediately he saw the heavens opened and the Spirit descending upon him like a dove; and a voice from heaven: 'Thou art my beloved Son; with thee I am well pleased'.   (Mark 1:10,11)

Mark observes that *Jesus saw*. It was the inner eye, the eye of love that saw; and Jesus realized in the Spirit that he was the Son of the Father.

We know little of what happened when Jesus went alone into the mountains to pray; but the Gospel story leads me to believe that those nights were spent in loving communion with the Father in the Spirit and in intercession for the world. Perhaps his prayer was sometimes like that of Gethsemane and at other times like that of Mount Tabor; but in either case it was dominated by love for his Father, a love which reaches a climax in those mystical chapters of the Fourth Gospel where Jesus speaks of the indwelling of the Son in the Father: Jesus is dwelling in his disciples and his disciples dwell in him and all are dwelling in God and God is dwelling in all. These are remarkable chapters. If we read them again and again we may find in ourselves that consciousness which is at the same time differentiated and undifferentiated, the consciousness which grasps unity and diversity at the same time. For Jesus prays 'that they may be one; even as thou, Father, art in me, and I in thee, that they also may be in us' (John 17:21). They are to be one, perfectly one, as Jesus is one with the Father. And yet they are not one, for the Father and the Son are different persons. I myself believe that this experience of unity in diversity and of diversity in unity is the core of the Christian mystical experience. And it can only be attained through love.

And so the life of Jesus is the working out of this relationship with the Father at whose command he lays down his life. It is a loving relationship which passes through its final stage of purification in a dark night of the soul when Jesus cries out: 'My God, my God, why hast thou forsaken me?' (Matthew 27:46). After this comes the resurrection and the sending of the Spirit.

IV

The conclusion, then, is that in the updating and modernizing of mystical theology the first step is a return to the Scriptures and, in particular, to the Gospel. Here we will find the mystical experience and the mystical teaching of Jesus of Nazareth. On this the whole structure of Christian mysticism is built. This was the food which nourished the Christian mystics; this was the fountain from which they drank. Mystics like St John of the Cross read and reread and re-read the Scriptures until Christ began to live his life in them.

For, as I have already indicated, Christian mysticism is nothing else than the process of becoming Christ – of living with him, of dying with him, of rising with him. Or of allowing him to live in us, to die in us, to rise in us. Jesus of Nazareth who lived and died in that little colony of the Roman Empire called Palestine wishes to relive his life in us – in Japan, in America, in India, in Europe, in Africa – in another time and another culture. For the mystics this was not just theory. They knew and deeply experienced that their lives were gradually dominated by the power of the resurrection (if I may borrow Paul's phrase) and that they were being transformed into Christ. Augustine in a different context will say that Peter baptizes but, in fact, it is Christ who baptizes: he is the principal agent in all we do. Others will say that Christ prays to the Father in me, suffers in me, dies in me – he sees through my eyes, listens through my ears, loves through my heart, blesses through my hands. 'It is no longer I who live but Christ who lives in me' (Galatians 2:20). Now the eye of love is no longer my eye but the eye of Christ who sees through my eyes and looks with compassion on the world.

Obviously, a mystical theology based on the Bible will be specifically Christian. As such, it will be the basis for dialogue with the mysticism of non-Christian religions. For, as I have already pointed out, Buddhism has its mystical theology based on the experience of the Buddha and on the Buddhist scriptures – based on the experience of becoming a Buddha. When Jesus and the Buddha meet in their disciples, real mystical dialogue will have begun.

At the same time, I believe it is also possible to sketch the beginnings of a mystical theology which will be common to both Christianity and Buddhism. About this I will speak later in this book.

5. *Mysticism in Theology*

I

I have spoken about mystical theology. But theology is broader than just mystical theology; and in this chapter I would like to discuss the role of mysticism in the vast and complex discipline which we call theology today. My contention will be that mystical experience is, and has to be, the very core of authentic theology. So it was in antiquity when theology was, in the wise words of Anselm of Canterbury, 'faith searching for understanding' (*fides quaerens intellectum*). The great theologians of primitive Christianity (that is to say, those who built Western civilization and whose works are vibrantly alive today) were men of faith, living faith, mystical faith. While their outer eyes pored over tomes and manuscripts and sacred books, their inner eye 'beheld his glory, glory as of the only Son from the Father' (John 1:14). In other words they were deeply enlightened people; and they tried to express – inadequately and imperfectly as they well knew – the wisdom they perceived with the inner eye. They knew, of course, that this vision could never be satisfactorily expressed in words; yet they did their best. As for Thomas, that wise and enlightened man, he finally protested that all his writings were as straw compared with the vision he perceived with the eye of love.

II

Let me start with St Paul. His mystical experience began on the road to Damascus when he fell in love with the Risen Jesus: 'Saul, Saul, why do you persecute me?' (Acts of the Apostles 9:4). Prior to this Saul had held the garments of the young men who stoned Stephen. He had seen that face which was like the face of an angel; he had heard that voice which cried: 'Lord, do not hold this sin against them' (Acts of the Apostles 7:60). Divine love, no doubt, was working in his unconscious before that flash of light which brought about the epoch-making conversion on the road to Damascus. This is the *metanoia*; this is the great turning-point; this is the death and resurrection – when Saul becomes Paul. Later he is to look back on this experience and see what an earth-shaking revolution took place in his life. His whole value system changed. Whereas he had been proud to be a Pharisee, a Hebrew of the Hebrews, a meticulous observer of the law, a persecutor of the Church, now all this is loss. 'Indeed I count everything as loss because of the surpassing worth of knowing Christ Jesus my Lord' (Philippians 3:8). For Paul to know Christ is to love him, to be united with him – to be united with him not in a static but in a dynamic way: 'That I may know him and the power of his resurrection, and may share his suffering, becoming like him in his death, that if possible I may attain the resurrection from the dead' (Philippians 3:10).

And so Paul's mysticism is one of action. There is no evidence that he spent long hours on his knees and I cannot imagine him sitting in the lotus – though he doubtless had lengthy periods of silence, of inner silence, in his journeys by sea and land as well as in the quiet of a prison cell. But Paul's union with Christ is dynamic in such wise that he suffers with Christ and dies with him. All through his letters the same idea recurs: with Christ I am nailed to the Cross. The whole drama of the life of Christ is not only a historical event, it is also an event which is taking place in Paul. 'It is no longer I who live, but Christ who lives in me' (Galatians 2:20). Indeed, the words 'in Christ' appear one hundred and sixty-four times in the Pauline writings. They are no mere metaphor but describe a real experience: the Church fathers compare Paul's, and our, immersion in Christ to the drop of water which falls into the wine or the glowing iron or coal which becomes part of the fire. But I believe that Pauline mysticism reaches its zenith when the great apostle realizes that he is a son and calls out 'Abba, Father!'.

The point I wish to make here, however, is that while Paul heard about Christ and 'received' the good news from apostles and eyewitnesses, he also met Christ, he was involved with Christ, he lived the good news in his busy life. And this shines through his theology: it is a theology which wells up from the depths of his powerful, inner experience. He writes about original sin as one who experiences original sin; he writes about redemption as one who experiences redemption; he writes about the death and resurrection of Jesus as one who experiences the death and resurrection of Jesus within himself; he writes about the Spirit as one who has received the Spirit; he calls God Father knowing that the Spirit of Jesus within is calling out: 'Abba, Father!'; he speaks of the love of Jesus as one who experiences the love of Jesus. In short, the theology of Paul is based not only on a historical event in the past but also on a living mystical experience in the present. This is what I mean when I say that mystical experience is the core of authentic theology.

III

Now as centuries pass new problems arise within Western Christianity and great theologians appear to solve them. Their task is to explain the Gospel in the language of their times and in the new culture which is being formed. And so a new theological vocabulary is forged and fresh insights are obtained. For the first time theologians use Hellenistic words like *Trinity*, *essence*, *nature*, *person*. These words are not found in the New Testament but they are necessary, even indispensable, in the new age. The theologians who use them know very well, like Paul, that they are dealing with mystery, they are trying to express the inexpressible, they are speaking about a reality which transcends formulations of any kind. But the Gospel has to be restated; a new theology has to be formed.

The question I wish to ask here, however, is: How did the great theologians of antiquity come to elaborate the new theology? Where did they get their knowledge? Whence came the inspiration and wisdom of Clement and Irenaeus and Gregory and Athanasius and Augustine? Did they just learn their theology from books?

Well, of course they studied. They read and reread the Bible, they knew the tradition of their forebears, they absorbed the culture of their times and studied the works of their adversaries. They were men of great learning. But they were also mystics and saints. And the secret of their great theological achievement was not their learning but their contemplation; not their outer eye but their inner eye. Through their mystical experience, through their contemplative reading of the Bible, through the inner revelation which we call grace (does not Augustine speak of 'the master within', the *magister internus*?) they came to meet the Risen Jesus in a personal way just like Paul. They, too, travelled their road to Damascus; they, too, were united with Christ; they, too, died and rose. As I said about Paul so I can say about them – if they wrote about sin and redemption this was because they experienced these things in their lives. If they wrote about the love of God it was because they experienced the love of God as a living reality. Their theology reflected their faith, the living faith, the mystical faith that burned in their hearts – out of the fullness of their hearts they spoke and wrote.

But they wrote and spoke for contemporary people. It is indeed a characteristic of great religious personalities that they reflect the conflicts and sufferings, the joys and the anguish of the world in which they live. That world vibrates within them; they breathe its air; they feel its frustrations; they carry its cross. This has been true, I believe, in our own times of Mahatma Gandhi and Teilhard de Chardin and Thomas Merton. It was also eminently true of Augustine and Gregory and Bernard and Thomas. Their enlightenment was not just biblical; it was the Gospel experience lived out and made incarnate in the new culture and the new world. Consequently it was profoundly relevant for the men and women of their day.

Their theology, I have said, welled up from their mystical experience. But (and this is very significant) it also led to mystical experience. In this sense it can be called a spirituality. For the fathers of the Church and the early Christian writers had no mystical theology apart from their ordinary theological writings: they had no separate discipline to which they could attach the label 'spirituality'. Their theological treatises, even when they were apologetic in nature, were calculated to lead the reader to a relishing of the great mysteries of faith. Take, for example, the doctrine of the Trinity. Later generations, alas, looked on this as an attempt to reconcile the seemingly contradictory teaching of three persons in one nature. Not so Augustine and Thomas. For them the Trinity is the key contemplative experience in the Christian life: it is the experience I have when, divested of self and clothed with Christ, I offer myself to the Father in the Spirit for the salvation of the world. These words may sound complicated but the experience itself is simple: God is my Father: I am his son: the Spirit dwells in me, and I cry out: 'Abba, Father!'. In this experience I have a consciousness which is at once undifferentiated and differentiated. It is undifferentiated in that there is a total unity, identification with Jesus and through Jesus with the Father; and, on the other hand, it is differentiated in that I am not Jesus and Jesus is not the Father. The experience of the Trinity was very real for Thomas (as it has been very real for all the Christian mystics) but a sad situation was created some centuries after his death when unenlightened scholastics repeated his Trinitarian words without enjoying his Trinitarian mysticism. They grasped the conceptualization but not the enlightenment which inspired it.

For the great temptation of theology has always been to divorce itself from mystical experience and to wander off into irrelevant speculation. That is why we find writers like Thomas à Kempis somewhat lugubriously warning ambitious clerics that it is better to have compunction than to know its definition and asking what is the value of speculation about the Trinity if one is not pleasing to the Trinity. This was a very real problem in the Middle Ages; and it is a very real problem today. Particularly so, since in the last few centuries theology has been greatly preoccupied with controversial issues, has become extremely academic and has largely divorced itself from spirituality. Contemplative experience has been relegated to the pious writers of pious books while theology proper has addressed itself to more academic questions. This is scarcely a healthy situation; for a theology which is divorced from the inner experience of the theologian is arid and carries no conviction.[1]

IV

And now at the end of the twentieth century we again find ourselves at a great crossroads in the history of mankind. Such an age demands a new theology, a re-statement of the Gospel message, an answer to the peculiar problems that confront us. Yet the construction of such a theology is an extremely difficult and delicate task because we are aware that the old culture is dying but has not yet died and the new culture is coming to birth but has not yet been born. Caught in the middle and not knowing what will come next we wonder where to turn. For my purposes here, however, it is enough to recall two aspects of this new culture. First of all it will be, and already is characterized by what Bernard Lonergan calls 'the switch to interiority'. That is to say, the whole emphasis is, and will be, on the inner world, the world of the mind, the human consciousness. Secondly, the new culture will certainly be a world culture profoundly influenced by all the great religions: Hinduism, Islam, Buddhism, Judaism as well as Christianity. In such a situation one of the great challenges to a new Christian theology will be mysticism, particularly oriental mysticism. How to meet this challenge?

From all that has been said in this chapter one might draw the conclusion that the primary need is for Christian theologians who are also mystics. It might be said that now, if ever, we need men of the stature of Paul and Augustine – we need men and women who will speak not only from a wealth of sound scholarship but also from a wealth of personal experience. It might be said that we need

[1] Let me add that Buddhism has precisely the same problem. The scholars are not always enlightened.

theologians who, while vibrating in unison with the modern world, have met Christ on the road to Damascus – only such people, it might be said, can build the new theology, speak to the modern world, speak to the Orient.

All this is very true and very fine. Yet I will refrain from drawing any conclusions of this nature. The reason is that from the time of Thomas à Kempis better men than I have been attempting to convert the theologians – and they have been conspicuously unsuccessful. The theologians remain unregenerate. Consequently I will confine myself to a more practical suggestion.

Is it not possible to elaborate a theological method which would put greater emphasis on *reflection on mystical experience*? Over the past two or three centuries, as I mentioned in the previous chapter, such reflection was relegated to a discipline of somewhat minor importance called *mystical theology* or *spiritual theology*; and while it is certainly useful to have such a separate discipline to treat of the practical problems of spiritual direction, the actual mystical experience should, it seems to me, occupy a more central position in the overall theological picture. In particular the mystical experience of the Trinity should be a central theme for theological reflection – for the doctrine of the Trinity comes out of the mystical experience of Jesus himself and looms large in the inner life of Paul and all the great Christian mystics. As I have said, the word 'Trinity' was not always used but the experience was always there.

Now I see the possibility of placing mystical experience in such an honoured position within the *method* elaborated by Bernard Lonergan. Here importance is given to research, interpretation of texts, history, doctrines; but when Lonergan comes to the foundation of theology he speaks of *reflection on conversion*.[1]

This conversion has a threefold nature: intellectual, ethical and religious. But here I need only mention religious conversion which is compared to the experience of a man falling in love with a woman or a woman falling in love with a man. The converted person is totally in love – 'in love without limits or qualifications or conditions or reservations' (Lonergan (1), p. 106). Here is how Lonergan speaks of religious conversion:

[1] 'As conversion is basic to Christian living, so an objectification of conversion provides theology with its foundations' (Lonergan (1), p. 130).

Religious conversion is being grasped by ultimate concern. It is other-worldly falling in love. It is total and permanent self-surrender without conditions, qualifications, reservations. But it is such a surrender, not as an act, but as a dynamic state that is prior to and principle of subsequent acts. It is revealed in retrospect as an under-tow of existential consciousness, as a fated acceptance of a vocation to holiness, as perhaps an increasing simplicity and passivity in prayer. It is interpreted differently in the context of different religious traditions. For Christians it is God's love flooding our hearts through the Holy Spirit given to us. It is the gift of grace . . .   (Lonergan (1), p. 241)

Now it can easily be seen that what Bernard Lonergan means by religious conversion and what I mean by mystical experience are very similar. There are, however, differences because while conversion involves a repudiation of the past or of some elements of the past, I do not see that mystical experience necessarily does so. But I do think that reflection on mystical experience together with reflection on conversion could be a foundation and basis of a theology of the future.

If this were so, pride of place would be given to the mystical experience of Jesus himself which, as I have repeatedly said, was primarily Trinitarian. Christianity indeed stems from the mystical experience or self-realization of Jesus, a self-realization which reaches a climax in his resurrection from the dead. That is to say, Jesus came to realize who he was. He saw that he was truly Son, the only-begotten Son, and that filled with the Spirit he could in a literal sense call God his Father and cry out: 'Abba, Father!'. He realized that all things had been delivered to him by his Father and that 'no one knows the Son except the Father, and no one knows the Father except the Son and any one to whom the Son chooses to reveal him' (Matthew 11:27). From the experience of his divine sonship came his vocation to reveal the love of the Father and to pray that 'the love with which thou hast loved me may be in them, and I in them' (John 17:26). That is, that the Spirit of love who was in him might be in them.

After the experience of Jesus we must reflect on that of Paul (again a Trinitarian experience), of the fathers of the Church and of the whole Christian community. I believe we will again and again find the same Trinitarian experience even in the hearts of the simple people who dare to say: 'Our Father . . .'.

Such a theology with its foundation in the mystical experience of Jesus and the Christian community is eminently suited to enter into dialogue with a modern world moving rapidly into the realm of interiority as well as with the great mystical religions of the East. For although Buddhists do not use my terminology, I believe that their whole philosophical reflection is founded on a consideration of the enlightenment of the Buddha, enlightenment attained beneath the Bodhi tree in Bodh Gaya and repeated in the lives of Buddhist patriarchs through the ages to the present day. A Christian theology which reflects on the mystical experience of Jesus and his disciples and the Christian community will be eminently suited to enter into dialogue with contemporary Buddhism.

6. *Mysticism in Religion*

I

I have spoken about a specifically Christian theology; and no doubt my readers, or some of them, are growing restless and asking: 'But what about Islam and Hinduism and Buddhism and Judaism? Surely these great religions have their profound mystical tradition which cannot be overlooked or omitted in any modern discussion of this subject. What about them? How do they fit into the mystical picture?'

Here let me recall my first chapter where I said that the great religions have as yet no common vocabulary or theological way of speaking and that this makes it necessary to take a stand within the framework of one religious tradition. Consequently I have spoken out of the Hebrew-Christian tradition of the West. And now while continuing to maintain this stand (and hoping that a Buddhist will approach this subject from a Buddhist standpoint and with a Buddhist vocabulary) I would like to sketch the beginnings of a mystical theology that will be universal in scope – that is to say, a mystical theology that will include the mystical experience of believers in all the great religions and, indeed, of those people who belong to no specific religion but have been endowed with profound mystical gifts. Such people there are. For mysticism is a human experience limited to no one religion: it is, I believe, the high point in man's search for fulfilment, authenticity and self-realization.

II

Let us, then, consider human life as a movement towards self-transcendence and authenticity through fidelity to the transcendental precepts:

Be Attentive
Be Intelligent
Be Reasonable
Be Responsible

It is by following these laws that one becomes fully human in one's thinking and in one's activity. Yet there is a more crowning precept which gives beauty and joy and fullness to human life. This is the precept:

Be in love (Lonergan (1), p. 13)[1]

Now it is my contention that a very radical fidelity to this last precept leads to mystical experience. And I draw the conclusion that as love is the most human of human activities, an activity for which the human heart was made, an activity in which men and women transcend themselves and become authentic, so mysticism, which is a question of love, is the most profoundly human activity. It is not a transcending of the human condition, as some authors have suggested, but a becoming more totally human. That is why it is a universal phenomenon and that is why one can speak of 'the universal call to mysticism'.

Assuredly mysticism is not achieved by human effort alone. Just as no sane man sits down and decides to fall in love with a woman, so no authentic human being calculatingly decides to fall in love with the infinite. Just as a man's love is elicited by the good in a woman, so unrestricted love is elicited by the footprints of the ox or the glimpse of the treasure hidden in the field. The call must always be there. And it *is* always there – because God shows no partiality. He wishes all men to be saved. He offers grace to everyone. It is in answering this call that men and women become truly human.

But before speaking about love, which is my main point here, let me discuss each of the transcendental precepts in its relationship to mysticism.

Be attentive! In Oriental meditation this attentiveness or awareness is of the utmost importance and there are many 'awareness exercises'. One can practise meditation simply by being aware of one's body or of one's breathing or of all the sensations that are going on inside oneself, a practice which sounds very easy but is extremely demanding. Or one can be totally aware of all the sights and sounds that are present here and now.

A variation of this is found in Zen. I can sit in the lotus posture

[1] See also p. 268 where Lonergan speaks of 'total surrender to the demands of the human spirit: be attentive, be intelligent, be reasonable, be responsible, be in love'.

just listening (that is, being totally attentive) to the flow of the river or the thunder of the waterfall. Here I am, sitting in total attentiveness or awareness. This in itself may bring profound interior peace and unification. But I can go one step further and, as I listen to those outer sounds, I can focus my attention inwardly by asking the question:

'Who is listening?'

Quietly sitting, I let go of all discursive reasoning, all thinking, all concepts and images; I keep asking myself this question, endlessly asking this question, with my attention focused not on the exterior object but on *myself as listening*.

Now it may happen that, if I practise this meditation for many hours or even for many days and weeks, I will come to a shattering enlightenment which fills me with joy and exaltation, liberating me from craving and anxiety. I may experience a timeless moment of illumination. *This is an experience not of the river nor of the waterfall but of my true self*; and it has come while I am faithfully practising the first two transcendental precepts: *Be attentive, be intelligent.* What a wonderful thing! I have broken out of the confines of my little ego. I have burst the bonds that imprisoned me in myself and have emerged from a habitat to a universe. Zen literature speaks enthusiastically about such experience: we hear of people who reach deep enlightenment just by listening. It is all very wonderful. But is it mysticism?

The answer is: No. For it is not knowledge that comes from love. It is, of course, a great triumph of the human spirit. One should never belittle such illumination. But it is no more than the first step on the road to authenticity.[1]

After having had this illumination, however, I may go one step further and make an affirmation or judgement. If I am Occidental, I may say: 'Being is!'. If I am Oriental, I may say 'Not a thing is!'. But in either case I have now transcended myself by making an

---

[1] Let me add, however, that the person who practises this kind of meditation may happen to be a mystic; he may well have in his heart an unrestricted love – which will then flower and develop through this exercise. What I am saying here is that *in itself* this great illumination is not mysticism as I have defined the word. For elaboration of this subject see 'Toward a Transcultural Philosophy' by J. Eduardo Perez Valera, *Monumenta Nipponica*, vol. XXVII.

objective judgement that reality exists or does not exist independently of myself. This may sound dull and drab and commonplace; but philosophers agree that the profound realization that *being is* can be an earth-shaking experience. It can be an intellectual conversion – 'a personal philosophical experience of moving out of a world of sense and arriving, dazed and disorientated for a while, into a universe of being' (Lonergan (2), p. 79). Aristotle speaks of such experiences of contemplation when man is like God and rises to the heights of spiritual attainment. This has come about from fidelity to the third transcendental precept: *Be reasonable*. Again, it is a great experience, but not mysticism.

But let us go one step further. Besides judgements about being there are judgements of value, when I affirm that something is good in itself irrespective of the pleasure or satisfaction it gives me. And perhaps I make this affirmation at the cost of liberty or life. I follow the voice of conscience rather than the lure of money and success; I choose duty rather than personal satisfaction. Here is the noble judge of ancient Rome who out of loyalty to country sentences his son to death. This is moral self-transcendence; it is fidelity to the fourth transcendental precept: *Be responsible*.

This again is a triumph of the human spirit. Here one transcends self even more than before and at much greater cost. Here one moves even closer to self-realization and authenticity. This may entail a great ethical conversion which brings immense joy in the midst of suffering. But is it mysticism?

Again the answer is: No. In itself it is not mysticism unless (as will frequently happen) the man who makes such a great decision is also drawn on by love. But in itself it is a moral, and not a religious, achievement.

III

The fifth transcendental precept is: *Be in love*. For besides striving to be attentive and intelligent and reasonable and responsible, men and women fall in love. They fall in love with one another and they fall in love with the infinite: that is to say, they fall in love without reservation or restriction. 'Being in love with God, as experienced, is being in love in an unrestricted fashion. All love is self-surrender, but being in love with God is being in love without limits or qualifications or conditions or reservations' (Lonergan (1), pp. 105, 106). This is authentic religious experience (I do not yet speak of mysticism proper) and it only arises in answer to an invitation or call from the Spirit who floods our heart with his love. The Hebrew-Christian tradition formulates it very clearly as the core and centre of religious experience: the Gospel looks back to Deuteronomy when it says: 'You shall love the Lord your God with all your heart, and with all your soul, and with all your strength, and with all your mind; and your neighbour as yourself' (Luke 10:27). Yet such unrestricted love is not limited to Judaism and Christianity.

But let me select some significant characteristics of this religious, unrestricted love.

First of all, it is a universal love from which one's enemies are not excluded. Moreover, it is incarnational in that it is not love of God divorced from love of the world. Rather it is the love about which I spoke in connection with Mother Teresa of Calcutta and Mahatma Gandhi and Ignatius of Loyola. It is the love which prompts good Samaritans everywhere to pick up the destitute and dying in the streets, to help the underprivileged, to give a glass of water to the little one. And yet at other times this same love may drive a person to leave everything for a life of solitude in a cave in the Himalayas or a hut in the desert.

And yet it should be noted that when I say unrestricted love I do not mean perfect love. I simply mean a love that goes on and on and on, just as man's knowledge and questioning go on and on and on. But, I repeat, it is never perfect in this life: authenticity is never fully achieved. The person with this unrestricted love has his conflicts and struggles, his imperfection and anguish, his neurosis and fear. He has his moments of betrayal and failure and sin. All this is part of that human adventure which is a love affair with the infinite. It is part of the experience of being in love.

Yet another aspect of this love (and one which is of supreme importance for the understanding of mysticism) is that it has eyes which see. In other words it is a love which necessarily brings enlightenment. And *the knowledge born of religious love* I call faith (Lonergan (1), p. 115). This is an obscure knowledge which dwells in the heart of the simplest person who loves God.

Such is the unrestricted love and such is the faith which lie at the heart of authentic religious experience.

But now let me come to mysticism.

This inner light of faith, this knowledge born of religious love, leads one to the outer revelation, the outer word of scripture and sacrament and community. Here it is nourished, here it develops and grows until eventually it enters a cloud of unknowing or a dark night. Now, while it continues to be nourished by the exterior revelation it *turns into naked faith, dark faith, pure faith. And this is mysticism.* It is naked because it is no longer clothed in thoughts and images and concepts; it is dark because it does not see clearly; it is pure because it is unmixed with concepts which (when applied to the divine) always contain an element of imperfection. It differs from ordinary faith only in the intensity of its nakedness, its darkness and its purity.

The Western mystics speak constantly of this naked faith. Especially valuable here is *The Book of Privy Counselling*, that little gem composed by the anonymous author of *The Cloud*, which opens with an exhortation to abandon all thoughts, good thoughts as well as evil thoughts, and continues with the words: 'See that nothing remains in your conscious mind save a *naked intent* stretching out towards God' (Johnston (1), ch. 1). And later in the same first chapter the author writes:

> This awareness, stripped of ideas and deliberately bound and anchored in faith, shall leave your thought and affection in emptiness except for a naked thought and blind feeling of your own being.   (Johnston (1), ch. 1)

And so this English author continues to exhort his disciple to remain naked, even when his faculties clamour to be clothed in thoughts, because only in naked faith is found security and freedom from error.

Now the point I wish to make here is that this naked faith is found in all the great religions. In Islam, in Hinduism, in Buddhism, and in Judaism we find people who love without restriction; who are filled with this exquisite wisdom which flows from religious love. They all speak of nakedness and darkness and emptiness and silence. And mystics of the great religions understand one another very well: they grasp intuitively, sometimes in a flash, the naked faith and the mystical solitude which dwells in the heart of the other.

Be it noted, however, that I am not saying that the naked faith in the heart of a Hindu and a Buddhist and a Christian is always the same. This no one can say; this no one knows. What we can say, however, is that there is a recognizable similarity between the naked faith of the Hindu and the Buddhist and the Christian and that it is

the gift of the same God. Hence it is the very best basis for ecumenical, if silent, encounter between the members of the great
religions.

Having said this, however, I am aware that this whole matter may
make some of my readers uneasy (some people rightly fear an over-
simplified syncretism) so let me elaborate first on the question of
love, then on the question of faith, and finally let me state my views
on the role of Jesus Christ in this mystical process which exists in all
the great religions.

IV

I have spoken of unrestricted love as the heart of authentic religious
experience in all the great religions. But I can foresee that some of
my readers may object that Buddhism says little or nothing about
love. Or they may object that being in love without restriction im-
plies the existence of a personal God. After all, it will be argued, if I
am in love I must be in love with somebody. If I am in love without
restriction I must be in love with a transcendent God. But, as everyone knows, Buddhism does not talk about God, much less about a
personal God. So I may be asked: 'Are you excluding Buddhism
from the mystical, and indeed from the religious, experience which
you call universal?'

In answer to this I would first of all agree that a Buddhist would
not ordinarily use my terminology: he would not speak about God
nor would he say much about love and about mysticism. But, as I
have repeatedly said, I am forced to use this terminology because we
have no theological way of speaking that applies to both religions.

If, however, we get beyond terminology and look carefully at the
reality towards which it points, then we will see that the Buddhist
mystics were what Westerners would call men and women in love.
It is true, of course, that they were not at all clear about the object
of their love. While Jews and Christians give a name to the object
and source of their love, the Buddhist resolutely refuses to name it.
Hence he will speak about 'nothing' but this nothing does not mean
that 'no thing is there' as I shall point out in a later chapter.

Furthermore, it is important to remember that if Buddhist
mystics are not clear about the object of their love, Christian
mystics are not clear either. For them God is not a clear-cut object
but a loving presence which they obscurely sense. They feel that they
are in a cloud of unknowing, crying out to a God whom they love but

cannot see. And at times even this loving presence is withdrawn and they are left crying out in the night of naked faith. Only from revelation can they say that the emptiness in which they find themselves is the love of a benevolent Father who wraps them in His tender care.

There can be no doubt: the Buddhist mystic, like his Christian counterpart, is passionately and unrestrictedly in love. In the history of Japanese Buddhism we find saints, and plenty of them, who braved the stormy seas to go to China in search of enlightenment. They tramped from temple to temple in search of a master. They sat for days and nights in the lotus posture. They endured heat and cold, hunger and thirst, scolding and beating. And this they did with joyful hearts. What can we say except that they were in love? They were drawn by someone or something they did not know. They loved without clear knowledge of the object of their love. And once enlightened, they had a limitless compassion for all sentient beings. Read the Buddhist sutras, read the *Lotus Sutra* and you will find tremendous and overflowing compassion in the heart of the bodhisattva – and this is not a vague and formless love but a great spiritual passion which is directed towards the tiniest and most insignificant being who crosses his path. The bodhisattva is in love with everyone he meets. This is unrestricted love. This is mysticism.

V

A second objection which may arise is that I have spoken about faith without differentiating sufficiently between Buddhist and Christian and Hindu and Jewish faith. How can one say that faith is the basis for ecumenical dialogue when there are, in fact, so many different kinds of faith?

And in answer to this I would like to distinguish between faith and belief. (Lonergan (1), p. 118ff).

In religious experience it is possible to distinguish between a superstructure which I shall call belief and an infrastructure which I shall call faith. The superstructure is the outer word, the outer revelation, the word spoken in history and conditioned by culture. The infrastructure, on the other hand, is the interior word, the word spoken to the heart, the inner revelation. It was of this that Jesus spoke when he said to Peter: 'Blessed are you, Simon Bar-Jona! For flesh and blood has not revealed this to you, but my Father who is in heaven' (Matthew 16:17). Here the Father speaks directly to the heart of Peter. Or again Jesus says: 'No one can come to me unless the Father who sent me draws him' (John 6:44). Read the Gospel and you find Jesus bumping into faith in the most unexpected places – people have faith without knowing clearly the object of their faith like the blind man who exclaims: 'And who is he, sir, that I may believe in him?' (John 9:36). Such is the inner word uttered by the Holy Spirit who floods our hearts with his love.

Now this inner light of faith is not the prerogative of Christians alone, for God loves all men and desires them to be saved (1 Timothy 2:4). Consequently this inner light shines in the hearts of all men and women of good will who sincerely search for the truth, whatever their religious profession. And it is precisely this which binds together Jew and gentile, Hindu and Buddhist, Christian and Moslem. This is an inner gift which at first is, so to speak, formless – that is, prior to any outer cultural formulation – and which often lives in the hearts of the most unsuspecting people who could never formulate it in words.[1]

At the risk of digressing for a moment let me say that this distinction between inner faith and outer belief throws light on our contemporary religious plight. We constantly hear talk about the crisis of faith in the modern world. But in the terminology which I have chosen our crisis is not one of faith but of belief. What is called into question today is the cultural superstructure with its myriad of beliefs. But there is plenty of evidence to support the view that the inner light of faith is as strong as ever in the modern world. Perhaps more than at any time in history men and women today are searching for the authentic superstructure, for the outer belief that will satisfy their inner longing for the infinite. But to return to my main point.

I have indicated that while the great religions differ in their beliefs their members can be deeply united in faith. But one should not conclude from this that the outer word of belief is unimportant. Not so. For the inner gift of faith always seeks outward expression. In itself it is imperfect and incomplete. Again let me quote Bernard Lonergan on the bridegroom and the bride:

One must not conclude that the outward word is something incidental. For it has a constitutive role. When a man and a

[1] Although formless, this is not the naked faith or mysticism of which I have spoken. It is the seed from which the flower of naked faith is eventually born.

woman love each other but do not avow their love, they are not yet in love. Their very silence means that their love has not reached the point of self-surrender and self-donation. It is the love that each freely and fully reveals to the other that brings about the radically new situation of being in love and that begins the unfolding of its life-long implications. (Lonergan (1), p. 112)

The inner light, then, leads to the outer revelation and is nourished by it. Put concretely in a Christian context the inner prompting of the Spirit leads us to the Word so that we cry out: 'Jesus is Lord' (Romans 10:9) with the realization that the God who speaks to the heart also speaks through history. And in other religions also the inner light of the Spirit (again I use the Christian term) leads people to recognize the working of the same Spirit in their history. And when this happens there is an interplay between the inner faith and outer belief – there is a marriage and a fullness of religious experience. It is through this that the naked faith about which I have spoken is finally born. Mysticism could never mature and develop without the exterior word.

Finally I promised to say a word about the role of Jesus Christ. Let me, then, state briefly my own belief.

I have spoken of an inner revelation, a gift of faith, an interior word offered to all men and I have said with Paul that God does not show partiality. This I believe is true. Yet I also believe that this inner grace is offered to all, thanks to the death and resurrection of Jesus Christ who is 'the true light that enlightens every man' (John 1:9). In other words, the inner light of faith is not unrelated to Christ but is his gift to all men. 'For there is one God, and there is one mediator between God and men, the man Christ Jesus, who gave himself as a ransom for all . . .' (1 Timothy 2:5,6).

I am aware that in taking this position I may sound unecumenical in that I give to Jesus Christ a unique role which I cannot accord to the founders of other religions even when I esteem them profoundly. But, after all, this is my belief, and ecumenism can only grow and develop when the members of the great religions are honest and faithful to their deepest convictions. Perhaps the matter could be stated more positively by saying that the Risen Jesus who sits at the right hand of the Father belongs to all men and to all religions. No one religion, even Christianity, can claim to understand 'the unsearchable riches of Christ' (Ephesians 3:8). That is why we need one another so that by dialogue and mutual help our partial knowledge may become more complete.[1]

More could be said about the relation of Jesus Christ to the founders of other religions but this must be postponed to a later time. Let me now speak more concretely about the Christian encounter with Buddhism.

[1] It should also be noted that there are two senses of the word mediation. There is the traditional doctrine according to which all graces are *mediated* through the death and resurrection of Jesus Christ. On the other hand, in the theology of Bernard Lonergan mediation is usually *a mediation of meaning*. And in this sense Christ is hardly the mediator for non-Christians since he mediates no meaning, or at least not the fullness of Christian meaning, to them. Hence Lonergan writes: 'What distinguishes the Christian, then, is not God's grace, which he shares with others, but the mediation of God's grace through Jesus Christ our Lord' (Lonergan(2), p. 156).

7. *Encounter with Buddhism (1)*

I

More than a millennium has elapsed since Christian Nestorian missionaries met Pure Land Buddhists in central China. How much mutual influence was then exerted is an open question to which scholars have not yet found a satisfactory answer. But since that time there has been constant contact (sometimes friendly but more often unfriendly) until today the two religions face one another like two great giants. What will happen next?

In this historic situation two attitudes of mind are apparent. The first is dominated by the question: *Who is going to win?* After all, Christian missionaries have ardently carried the Gospel to the East, while Buddhist missionaries have equally ardently carried the *dharma* to the West. Now the two religions, already world-wide communities with followers everywhere, look like two *sumo* wrestlers (this is the image used by a Japanese Buddhist writer) quietly confronting one another in the ring. Who is going to win? This kind of question preoccupied even the great soul of Teilhard de Chardin who confidently predicted the victory of the West. It is also broached by Mircea Eliade who indicates that the West is being slowly dominated by the East. Alas, poor Yorick! And does the West again need three hundred Spartans to stand in the pass of Thermopylae and save it from destruction?[1]

I do not think so. For a second attitude of mind is possible. We can view the encounter of religions in the wider context of a human race searching for world unity and desperately realizing that it must find unity or perish. In such circumstances the challenge confronting the two wrestlers is not to throw one another out of the ring but to join hands, to give the lead, to show the way, to become the centre of a movement towards unity and peace. Assuredly this is no easy task (it would be much easier to fight) but is it not particularly the challenge thrown down before that wrestler who owes allegiance to one who prayed for unity – who prayed that his disciples might

[1] For Teilhard see *Towards the Future* (Collins, London 1975, p. 145). Eliade (1), p. 100.

be one, perfectly one, and that this unity might be a sign of the unity of all mankind?

II

In Japan (the Asian country with which I am most familiar) the relationship between Christianity and Buddhism was somewhat stormy until recent times. In the 1890s, it is true, some orthodox Buddhists met in friendly, if uneasy, dialogue with a group of orthodox Protestant Christians; but for Catholic Christians no deep encounter took place until the late 1960s when the Second Vatican Council had already ushered in a new age.

Preoccupied with problems of international peace and world unity, the Council could not fail to see that dissension between religions was a scandal whereas unity would be a beacon light to the whole world. And so we find stress on unity: 'For all peoples comprise a single community and have a single origin . . . One also is their final goal' (Abbot, pp. 660-1). And this was followed by the clear assertion that the Church rejects nothing that is good, that she honours and respects the great religious traditions, that she recognizes the Spirit of God working in ancient cultures prior to the preaching of the Gospel. And this is rounded off by an exhortation to 'acknowledge, preserve and promote the spiritual and moral good found among these men as well as the values in their society and culture'.

At first it all sounded revolutionary, even scandalous. 'Are we not encouraging people in their error?' it was asked. Yet the Council's message was nothing less than an answer to the prayer, the toil, the research of many missionaries and theologians who for long had been impressed by the undeniable goodness and truth and beauty of the indigenous religions in their adopted countries. Moreover, it was the continuation of an even older tradition which held that Yahweh made a covenant not only with Israel but with the whole human race when he pointed to the multi-coloured rainbow and spoke to Noah: 'Behold I set my bow in the cloud, and it shall be a sign of the covenant between me and the earth' (Genesis 9:13). Such an appreciation of the inherent goodness of the human race is also found throughout the Gospel of St Luke and in the Church fathers, notably Gregory of Nyssa who claims that the collective human race, not just the individual soul, is created in the image of God.

From this it is not difficult to conclude that there is a revelation to all authentic religions and to all peoples. No one is deserted by God; no nation is without its divine gift; and in this sense every nation is a chosen people. With this we can also definitively bid farewell to the outside-the-church-no-salvation way of thinking as well as to exaggerated ideas about the ravages of original sin and the *massa damnata* which sits in outer darkness. We can have a more optimistic view of God's grace offered to all men.

And so now, it seems to me, the authentic Christian position is to encourage good wherever one finds it – even if it exists in an apparently rival camp. If something is good it is the gift of the same Yahweh who set his bow in heaven as a sign of his covenant with the human race. If something is good it belongs to the Christian. That is why Paul can tell the Corinthians that everything belongs to them. 'For all things are yours, whether Paul or Apollos or Cephas or the world or life or death or the present or the future, all are yours; and you are Christ's; and Christ is God's' (1 Corinthians 3:23). That is why he can tell the Colossians to enjoy everything good in life: 'Finally, brethren, whatever is true, whatever is honourable, whatever is just, whatever is pure, whatever is lovely, whatever is gracious, if there is any excellence, if there is anything worthy of praise, think about these things' (Colossians 4:8).

How far this is from the anguishing who-is-going-to-win frame of mind! No. Let those two *sumo* wrestlers shake hands. Let them work together in service of mankind. It would be no fun to watch one throw the other out of the ring while the excited crowd roared with thunderous applause or lifted hands of despairing grief.

III

Over the past few decades dialogue has flourished in the modern world and has taught us some worthwhile lessons. In particular dialogue between Christians has taught us three lessons which I would like to mention before applying them to the wider dialogue with Buddhism.

First of all, we see the immense wisdom of Gamaliel who, when the apostles were dragged before the Sanhedrin prudently counselled the group: '. . . keep away from these men and let them alone; for if this plan or this undertaking is of men, it will fail; but if it is of God, you will not be able to overthrow them. You might even be found opposing God' (Acts of the Apostles 5:38,39).

Underlying these words is an enormous faith in the ultimate

victory of truth. We do not need to hound error or to persecute those whom we consider erroneous. Neither need we feel threatened by others. The truth will prevail since it is of God. If only Christians had appreciated the wisdom of these words a few centuries ago! How much suffering would have been spared!

A second point we have learned is that unity is achieved more quickly and more deeply by common prayer than by discussion. This latter frequently leads to bitterness, controversy and anger whereas prayer unites. Prayer in common reminds us all that union is a gift of God and cannot be achieved by human effort alone. Furthermore, prayer is closely associated with forgiveness. 'And whenever you stand praying, forgive, if you have anything against anyone; so that your Father also who is in heaven may forgive you your trespasses' (Mark 11:25). And Matthew's Gospel adds: 'But if you do not forgive men their trespasses, neither will your Father forgive you your trespasses' (Matthew 6:15). Do not take these words as a threat, as though the Lord were warning those who do not forgive. They are no threat but a statement of the intrinsic nature of things. Lack of forgiveness renders prayer totally impossible because it erects a barrier between ourselves and others, between ourselves and God. While, on the other hand, prayer leads us to forgive and to receive forgiveness. The wounds of the past are healed – those deep wounds that have lived for centuries in the unconscious. The healing power of prayer has to be experienced to be understood.

A third lesson we have learned is that common action unites. In famine and in earthquake, in flood or in fire when Christians have united to fight against injustice or to help the poor they have experienced a bond of union and a friendship which has made them realize that they are one in Christ. It is indeed an interesting fact that any kind of common action, even sport, unites; and we all know that cracks appeared in the bamboo curtain when the ping-pong team went to China.

These three points, with necessary adaptation, are valid in Christian dialogue with Moslems and Jews. But what about Hindus and Buddhists? Here the problem is more delicate since the gap which separates us is much greater. Yet I believe that we can work towards union with these same three points as guidelines.

About the statement of Gamaliel I need not speak since it is clear that in dialogue Christians and Buddhists must recognize one another's position. But there is the question of prayer. Can Buddhists and Christians pray together?

If by prayer we mean intercession or thanks or praise to a Father who loves us, orthodox Buddhists are slow to accept any such practice since it seems incorrigibly dualistic and contrary to the sense of oneness on which their religious experience is built. Even Pure Land Buddhism which constantly calls on the name of the Buddha Amida ends up by saying that Amida is your own mind. That, at least, is what orthodox Buddhist scholars say – what precisely is in the mind of the simple people who invoke the name of Amida is another story – and they cannot accept the kind of intercessory prayer which exists in Judaism, Christianity and Islam.

I myself believe, however, that this difference is less formidable than appears at first sight. For the highest form of intercession is not simply dualistic. I invoke the God with whom I am one. It is like the prayer of Jesus who calls out, 'Abba, Father!' and yet claims that he and the Father are one. So we, through Jesus, are one with the God whom we invoke. I will speak about this in a later chapter and deal with its Trinitarian connotations. Here only let me say that at our present stage of dialogue this is still a hurdle; Buddhists do not accept prayer of intercession: I know of no case in which Buddhists and Christians pray together in this way.

However, even if common prayer of intercession is impossible, Christians and Buddhists can still have a *religious experience in common*. For example, we can sit together in silent and wordless meditation. And in such a situation we can feel not only the silence in our hearts but the silence of the whole group. Sometimes such silence will be almost palpable and it can unite people more deeply than any words.

Now you may ask: What precisely is this silence which is uniting you – Christians and Buddhists?

And I would answer, first of all that it is our common human nature. When we sit together in silent meditation, just being, we are experiencing our true selves at the existential level. We are all doing the same thing: just being. And this gives birth to a powerful unity.

But going one step further I would say that we are united at the level of faith. Remember that I distinguished between the superstructure of belief and the infrastructure of faith, and I said that this infrastructure is a formless inner light. Here we have it in practice. For here we have a situation in which the eyes are turned away from words and concepts and images to remain in empty faith. And do not think that such faith is the prerogative of Christians alone. Buddhists of all sects, including Zen, speak constantly about faith and its necessity. And when this faith flowers and develops into the naked faith which I have called mysticism then the union is deepest. This is the union of people who are in love without restriction or reservation and whose love has entered the cloud of unknowing. They are one at the centre of things; they are one in the great mystery which hovers over human life and towards which all religions point.

Here I have been speaking of Christian dialogue with those forms of Buddhism which concentrate on wordless meditation. But equally interesting is the dialogue with Pure Land Buddhism.

I have already spoken of the invocation of Amida. *Namu Amida Butsu*, meaning 'I take refuge in the Buddha Amida' or 'Honour to the Buddha Amida', is repeated again and again and again with the faith that through the merits and mercy of Amida one will be released from bad *karma* and reborn in the Pure Land. This form of Buddhism, little known in the West, was extremely widespread in Asia and was at one time the most popular form of Buddhism in Japan. Anyhow, a friend of mine, a committed Christian, has entered deeply into dialogue with Pure Land Buddhists by praying with them (I think prayer is the only word I can use) and by speaking to groups of young Buddhists on the beauty and power of faith. Her faith is in Jesus (she constantly recites 'the Jesus prayer') and their faith is in Amida. And this is quite clear to everyone. While with joy and gratitude they pray, 'I take refuge in Amida', she with equal joy and gratitude prays, 'I take refuge in Jesus'. It is almost an amusing situation. But here there is a beautifully-shared experience. A close bond of unity and love is established.

Here again is a situation which can be explained by distinguishing between faith and belief. There is profound union at the level of faith even when the belief seems completely different. This is the level at which we can all be in love without restriction, all possessing the wisdom which flows from love.

IV

Finally there is the question of common action. This brings us back to the two *sumo* wrestlers. Are they going to expend their energies in fighting one another or are they going to join hands to serve the world?

Let us remember that the aim of a religion is not to increase its own numbers but to serve the world and to promote the salvation of men. If we look back in history we can see that both Buddhism and Christianity (in spite of their defects) have always served their people by giving spiritual values to the culture of the time. In this way Christianity served and gave inspiration to the Hellenistic world, the medieval world, the renaissance world – a glance at the art and music and poetry of these times makes this clear. And anyone who passes through Asia getting even a superficial view of its ancient culture sees the great spiritual and cultural achievements of Buddhism. In both East and West the inner eye, the eye of love, has always been active, has always been beautiful and without it the cultural achievement would have been nil, or almost nil. 'So, if your eye is sound, your whole body will be full of light; but if your eye is not sound, your whole body will be full of darkness' (Matthew 6:22,23).

But now we are entering a new world which has largely rejected both Christianity and Buddhism. It is a world which, in spite of its incredible progress, is acutely aware of its spiritual poverty, its rootlessness, its insecurity, its superficiality. It is a world which is unable to handle problems of nuclear energy, peace and war; unable to cope with social injustice, racial discrimination, marital breakdown and fear of the future. It is a world which, for all its talk about democracy, needs leadership and looks for guidance. For it is a world from which despair is not absent. Who is to guide such a world? Who is to give it spiritual values?

Surely this task must be undertaken by Christians and Buddhists and the believers of all the great religions. This is the challenge to the wrestlers. No one religion can answer the needs of modern man. We must pool resources and insights so that together the great religions can offer the values of meditation, interiority, compassion, nonviolence, justice, peace, fidelity. Through co-operation in this great venture sincere believers of all religions can form friendship and community; they can travel the path of union.

8. *Encounter with Buddhism (2)*

I

I have said that believers of the great religions can best meet at the level of faith even when their beliefs are vastly different; and I have said that the deepest encounter will take place in the area of mysticism where we go beyond thoughts and concepts and images to a state of silent love. Here the conceptual superstructure is reduced to the minimum; here people remain in wordless union; here spirit meets spirit. Jews and Christians, Hindus, Buddhists and Moslems believe in the existence of a 'hidden power which hovers over the course of things and over the events of human life. (Abbot, p. 661). And when this infinite power is not just recognized but deeply experienced union is indeed profound.

But all this is not to say that discussion and exchange of ideas is useless. Far from it. We must eventually talk to one another with friendship and true desire to help. Let us remember that dialogue of some kind has existed between religions from the earliest times. There is no religion in the world which has not been influenced by other religions. Even Old Testament Judaism which was extremely careful to preserve its own unique insight was greatly influenced, we now know, by the surrounding religions. No need to speak here of Hindu influence on Buddhism or of how Christianity was influenced by Hellenism (the Dionysian story is one example of this) and how today all modern religions have received influence from Marxism, existentialism and the culture of our time.

Between the Reformation and the Second Vatican Council, it is true, Christianity in both its Protestant and Catholic form insulated itself carefully from outside influence – with the consequence that growth ceased. But now dialogue and exchange of opinion has developed into an art and we are faced with a period of tremendous progress: dialogue with science, dialogue with Oriental religions. We have learnt to meet and mutually explain our beliefs without thought of proselytizing, without exerting pressure on others, with complete equality and inner freedom. In dialogue both parties are free to take what they want and leave what they don't want.

Furthermore, exchange of ideas and mutual sharing can take

place in many areas: through liturgy, through spiritual literature, through conversation. Whereas at one time Christians were insulated from the holy books of other religions now they can discerningly read the *Bhagavad Gita*, the *Tao te Ching* and the Buddhist sutras. If these works contain a genuine insight into the nature of reality and the mystery of life, is it not legitimate and desirable for educated Christians discerningly to avail of this insight? And is it not also desirable that Buddhists and Hindus should avail of the treasures and insights of the Christian classics? Indeed, one interesting example of this is found in Mahatma Gandhi. Here was a Hindu with remarkable insight into the Sermon on the Mount which he brilliantly applied to social and political life. How many Christians have understood as profoundly as Gandhi the precepts to forgive one's enemy, to turn the other cheek, to give away one's cloak? How many Christians have understood as well as he did the power of suffering and of non-violence and of truth and of seeking first the kingdom of God and his justice? Gandhi confessed openly and frequently his debt to the Gospel; but he remained a Hindu. Similarly some modern Christians have had remarkable insight into the practice of Oriental meditation; they have seen in Buddhist and Hindu scriptures treasures which have astonished Buddhists and Hindus. Yet they remain Christians. And so the process of cross-fertilization goes on. I myself believe that the sharing of the Gospel, the sharing with others of 'the unsearchable riches of Christ' (Ephesians 3:8) is as relevant and imperative as ever. Only it must be done in a context of dialogue and never with force or constraint.

Obviously all this exchange of ideas has its problems and difficulties and dangers. At an ecumenical meeting I once attended, a Japanese Buddhist observed smilingly that we all feel the religious and cultural danger: we all feel threatened. And his remark was a bit like that of the little boy who observed that the emperor was wearing no clothes. For if we dialogue we must be prepared to change (otherwise why dialogue?) and for some people this change entails a profound psychological shock. They are sadly jolted. They feel that the rug has been pulled from under their feet or that they are adrift on a sea of insecurity. This is particularly true if the change affects not only outward things like structures and the externals of liturgy but the very way of thinking about God and Christ and redemption and original sin. And such violent change is taking place today not only because of the meeting of East and West but also because East and West are both facing the birth of an entirely new culture in the whole world. All this revolutionizes our society and our religious way of thinking until we begin to ask: 'But what are the limits of change? Can we go on changing for ever? Will we lose our identity as Christians or as Buddhists?' Is there a point at which we can face the movement towards change with the words: 'Thus far shalt thou go and no further?' This is a point to which I would like to give some consideration.

II

All authentic religion originates with mystical experience, be it the experience of Jesus, of the Buddha, of Mohammed, of the seers and prophets of the *Upanishads*. The founders speak of a realm of mystery that lies beyond the reach of thinking and reasoning and concepts of any kind, a realm about which one can only speak stammeringly and indirectly. They use expressions which they or their followers translate into words like Yahweh and God and Brahman and the Tao and the Buddha nature or whatever it may be. No one can have a clear and distinct idea of what these words mean: the reality to which they point lies hidden in a cloud of unknowing. 'No one has ever seen God' (John 1:18).

But being human we must try to express this great mystery in words and phrases and holy books as well as in liturgy and drama and dance and art of all kinds. This we do; but however rich and beautiful the words and descriptions, they never contain the reality. 'Eye has not seen nor ear heard, neither has it entered into the heart of man to conceive what God has prepared for those who love him' (1 Corinthians 2:9). The mystics are keenly aware of the inadequacy of words and phrases which try to formulate the mystery of life. That is why they are so often silent and say nothing. It is not that the formulations are wrong but that they are hopelessly inadequate to express this great mystery of which the mystic has had the tiniest existential glimmering.

Furthermore, any conceptual system or formulation in words is culturally and historically conditioned. That is to say, it takes on the cultural patterns of the society in which it was written. The Bible was written mainly by Jews with a Jewish way of thinking and a Jewish mode of expression. Augustine wrote from within a Hellenistic framework: he explains the Trinity and the Redemption to suit his age and to answer the questions of his day. So also does Aquinas. And so we have several formulations of the Christian message. Only today are we beginning to understand the full implications of 'historicity'. Now we realize that we can only understand Paul or Augustine or Aquinas or the theologians of the Reformation by studying the historical background out of which they wrote. It is useless to quote Augustine as a spokesman for modern Christianity without examining his cultural background. It is also impossible to come up with one formulation of Christianity which will last for all time. We may (and hopefully we will) find a formulation that will speak to the men and women of our age; but the next century will look for something different. They will not say our formulation was wrong; but they may say that it does not suit them and has to be modified or changed.

Viewed in this way we can see that in the area of formulation and conceptualization of doctrines as well as in the area of rites and structures, change is constantly taking place. Anything can change. There will always be reformulation, new insights, progress, new understanding of the great unchanging mystery which hovers over human existence.

And the moral from all this is that we must not become too attached to words and letters. Yes. There is a fine Buddhist saying that words and letters are like a finger pointing to the moon. If you want to see the moon, don't get too attached to that finger. Don't be attached to words and letters. Look out into the night for that reality to which they point.[1]

But the question, the sometimes agonizing question, remains: Is there anything I can cling to?

III

If we read the Bible we quickly discover that one thing is unchanging: the steadfast love of God. 'For the mountains may depart and the hills be removed but my steadfast love shall not depart from you, and my covenant of peace shall not be removed' (Isaiah 54:10). It is precisely here that the Jews find their security. The bride may play the harlot; the people may turn to the fleshpots; the heavens may collapse and the rivers run dry; but Yahweh will always love his people. And Paul is profoundly conscious of the fidelity of God. 'Let God be true though every man be false' (Romans 3:4). But for

---

[1] All this is not to deny that the formulations contain the truth, but only to point out that in true propositions there are relative elements. See Lonergan (2), p. 11ff.

him this love of God is 'in Christ Jesus Our Lord' (Romans 8:37). Nothing can separate us from this.

Now the steadfast love of God is a mystery. It can never be adequately described or delineated through any conceptual system. Moreover, its expressions are always changing – no one is more unpredictable than the God of Israel. In short, *the mystery of God's love can only be grasped through faith*. If we want to cling to anything we can only cling to faith. This is the message of Paul in Romans and he appeals to the example of Abraham.

I myself belong to a little dialogue group consisting of Buddhists and Christians of various denominations. One of our Japanese Christian members maintains strongly that our patron saint must be our father Abraham. Here is a patriarch who goes forth from his home and from his kindred. Where he is going he does not know; but he has faith, faith in the promise: 'I have made you the father of many nations' (Romans 4:17).

But the promise is a mystery of which Abraham's understanding is very imperfect. In fact he is quite baffled by the whole thing. It looks ridiculous yet 'he did not weaken in faith when he considered his own body, which was as good as dead because he was about a hundred years old, or when he considered the barrenness of Sarah's womb' (Romans 4:19). The promise seems even more absurd when he is ordered to kill Isaac. Surely the death of his only son will nullify everything! Yet 'no distrust made him waver concerning the promise of God, but he grew strong in his faith as he gave glory to God, fully convinced that God was able to do what he had promised' (Romans 4:20,21).

And so Abraham has great faith in a mystery which cannot be adequately formulated. If it is formulated the wording is imperfect and the reality is hidden. 'And I will make you a great nation, and I will bless you and make your name great . . . and by you all the families of the earth shall bless themselves' (Genesis 12:2,3). This promise is very mysterious and we do not yet know its full meaning and its implications. Some light is shed on it by the Mosaic covenant and by the new covenant predicted by Jeremiah and by the words of Jesus at the Last Supper. But it is still a mystery. The promise; the love of God; the old covenant; the new covenant – this is the great unchanging mystery which lies at the core of the Hebrew-Christian tradition.

Because of his faith Abraham had to abandon all security of any kind. Not only did he leave his home and kindred and country but he had to relinquish attachment to his only son. More than that, he had to be detached from the promise itself – because if Isaac was dead how could the promise be fulfilled? Abraham was left with nothing, with absolutely nothing. And this is pure faith, naked faith. This is mysticism.

Nor is it by accident that Paul cites Abraham as his model. Because Paul, too, has to abandon all security and all formulations of the law to carry the Christian message out of its Jewish framework into the Hellenistic world. What was Paul's old security? To be 'circumcised on the eighth day, of the people of Israel, of the tribe of Benjamin, a Hebrew born of Hebrews, as to the law a Pharisee, as to zeal a persecutor of the Church, as to righteousness under the law blameless' (Philippians 3:5). How important all this was for the young Paul! His religious adherence to the law and his cultural background were everything to him. But he had to give up all – 'for his sake I have suffered the loss of all things' (Philippians 3:8) – in order to move forward with faith in only Christ: 'that I may know him and the power of his resurrection' (Philippians 3:10). And so for Paul the whole Jewish framework of circumcision and the law collapsed, but his faith in the promise remained. He was a true son of Abraham.

All this may seem like a digression. But what I want to say is that our situation today is not unlike that of Abraham and of Paul and we must emulate their faith. We, too, have the promise. This time it is the promise of Jesus: 'I will be with you all days even to the end of the world' (Matthew 28:20). What precisely this promise entails we do not know. We will only know from day to day as it is revealed to us by the Spirit. Quite certainly we will get severe shocks because just as the promise to Abraham was fulfilled in a way he could never have imagined so will be fulfilled the promise to us. But of one thing we can be sure: it will be fulfilled in a more mysterious and wonderful and beautiful way than we can imagine. So with Abraham; so with us.

Let us remember, too, how at the Last Supper Jesus told his disciples that they could not understand his whole message immediately but that the Holy Spirit would guide them day by day and would direct and comfort and strengthen them. 'But the Counsellor, the Holy Spirit, whom the Father will send in my name, he will teach you all things and bring to your remembrance all that I have said to you' (John 14:26). Day by day as each new situation arises the

Spirit will direct us.

And so I reach the conclusion that the very question: 'What are the limits of change?' may even be an indication that we are clinging to words and letters, to plans and false securities; and all this may distract us from the important work of listening to the daily inspirations of the Spirit.

We live in an age which asks for faith, pure faith, naked faith, mystical faith. It is an age in which we accept the formulations but see their inadequacy; we believe in the doctrines but do not cling to the words; we respect the teaching of the past but are not attached to the modes of expression. This means that we are open to change. It means that there will be times when we must sing with St John of the Cross:

> With no other light or guide
> Than the one which burns in my heart
> (*Ascent*, Stanza 3)

Like Abraham we are going on a journey into darkness. In order that we may go to a place that we do not know we must go by a way that we know not. We do not know the place and we do not know the way. This may mean that we suffer some of the insecurity of Abraham and we may be visited by some of the dread which fell upon him: 'As the sun was going down, a deep sleep fell on Abram; and lo, a dread and a great darkness fell upon him' (Genesis 15:12). Like him we have faith in the steadfast love of God which lasts for ever.

IV

But there is one practical problem of dialogue which must sooner or later be confronted. Let me put it this way: Is it possible for a Christian, a committed Christian, to experience another religion from inside? Can dialogue go to such lengths?

This question could not have been asked twenty years ago but now with the new thinking about non-Christian religions it is not irrelevant. We know that Thomas Merton spoke of (shall we say soliloquized about the possibility of?) practising Oriental meditation in a Buddhist temple and under the direction of a Buddhist master; but death tragically intervened. He was, of course, misunderstood; and some people spoke foolishly of Merton's 'conversion to

Buddhism'. Yet other Christians, committed Christians, ask if confronted with Buddhism one is in an either-or situation. Can a Christian avail of the treasures and wealth of Buddhism from inside?

To this I would answer that quite certainly Christians can experience *some of the values of Buddhism* from within. If the Spirit is at work within Buddhism it would seem legitimate to enter discerningly and find his action. If in Buddhism there is an experience of the Absolute (and I believe there is) why cannot a Christian experience the Absolute through Buddhist categories?

The question usually asked, however, is: 'What about the role of Christ?' Or, as someone facetiously put it, do you leave Christ at the door of the temple with your shoes?

And to this I would answer with Paul that no authentic Christian can be separated from the love of Christ. If he enters the Buddhist temple he does so as a member of Christ – to grow in the Christ experience and to search for Christ who, he believes, is there in another way. This may mean that he leaves his thoughts and concepts and images of Christ at the door (just as a Buddhist leaves his thoughts and concepts and images of the Buddha at the door) but he does so to find Christ through other cultural categories, to meet the Risen Jesus, the universal man who belongs to all cultures. In fact, one of the great challenges confronting modern Christians is that of experiencing Christ in a non-Christian culture. Precisely because Christianity claims to be a universal religion we cannot shirk this challenge.

And yet, having said all this, I would quickly add that such a venture is for a few people who feel within themselves the vocation to a delicate path which demands much prudence and discernment. For the fact is that just now we do not know how much of Buddhism can be accepted by Christians; we do not know if there is incompatibility or, if there is, where it lies. We are at the beginning of a long, long journey. Consequently this pioneering work is not something to be undertaken lightly and in cavalier fashion. It may be the calling of some who have experienced Christ profoundly in their own culture and are willing to accept the cultural cross, the anguish and the conflict which necessarily accompanies any attempt to reconcile seeming contraries. This is the vocation of a few who have already seen the glory of Christ with the inner eye of love.

PART III

THE MYSTICAL JOURNEY

9. *The Call*

Mystical experience begins with an invitation. It is never something that we strive for by personal effort – or if we strive we must remember that our very striving is a gift. It is a call from beyond oneself. Sometimes this call is dramatic, as were the great inaugural visions of the prophets Isaiah and Jeremiah, or the flash of light that blinded Paul on the road to Damascus. At other times it is a secret and quiet call, a still small voice like that which spoke to Elijah, a voice that may have been alive in the heart since early childhood. Then this invitation is so delicate, so subtle, so unobtrusive that the recipient does not even realize that he has been called and has to be reminded: 'You did not choose me, but I chose you . . .' (John 15:16).

The futility of human effort and the necessity of a call is a note that is sounded in the mysticism of all the great religions. It is strikingly presented in the *Upanishads* where the Ultimate, called the Self (Brahman and Atman), is the one who chooses and calls: 'That Self cannot be attained by the study of the scriptures, nor by the intellect, nor by learning. He whom the Self chooses, by him, the Self can be attained' (Griffiths (2), p. 103). Assiduous study of the scripture, faithful practice of virtue, constant devotion to learning, practice in breathing, sitting and awareness – these things have value; but in the last analysis what matters is grace.

In Christianity, as we have already seen, mysticism begins and ends with the experience of being loved. 'We love, because he first loved us' (1 John 4:19). The secret of the energy and fire of Paul and Bernard and Teresa was not so much that they loved (this was secondary) as their conviction of being loved. So also the prophets. They are called from their mother's womb – that is to say, they are called without any merit on their part. 'Before I formed you in the womb I knew you . . .' (Jeremiah 1:5). This call is purely gratuitous. It does not come because Jeremiah is good but because God is good. And so the principal thing in the mystical life is not to love but to receive love, not to love God and man but to let yourself be loved by God and man. Don't put barriers in the way; don't put up a defence mechanism; let love come in – because human love is a response to divine love. This is the message of the First Epistle of St John. This is the key to mysticism.

Yet if there is a call and if we hear it, then ordinarily we answer. 'Then the Lord called, "Samuel! Samuel!" And he said, "Here I am!"' (1 Samuel 3:4). And so in the mystical life. But the answer (as I have already indicated) is also a gift. It is moreover a living and burning reality that arises in the human breast and can only be described in symbolical language. It is what St John of the Cross powerfully calls a 'living flame of love'; it is what the author of *The Cloud* calls a 'blind stirring of love'; it is a dark night and a cloud of unknowing; it is a quiet movement in the depths of one's being; it is a passionate being in love without restriction; it is the urgent longing which motivates the whole mystical journey:

> One dark night
> Fired with love's urgent longing
> – Ah, the sheer grace! –
> I went out unseen
> (*Ascent*, Stanza 1)

And so here we have an inner light which guides and directs. This light is the Holy Spirit.

All this is difficult to express in ordinary language and the mystics usually resort to symbols. Here let me refer to twelve symbolical pictures which describe the mystical journey as it was envisaged in ancient China. I choose these pictures because I believe they have universal validity and can apply equally well to Christians or Buddhists or anyone who is called to this mystical journey. I believe they illustrate the point I made earlier that mysticism is a deeply human experience found at all times and in all cultures.

The first picture depicts man lost in the woods and searching for a way out. This is life; this is the human condition; this is the situation in which we men and women find ourselves – we are lost in the woods and looking for a way out. (I might add, however, by way of digression that one could draw a picture antecedent to the first; and this would be of the man who is lost in the woods without knowing that he is lost. This is the most pitiable condition of all: the condition of the blind man who thinks he sees. The blind man who knows he is blind has already made progress. But, anyhow, no such picture exists in the Chinese series: it begins with man lost in the woods and desperately trying to get out.)

In the second picture, which is the one I wish to speak about here, he sees the footprints of the ox. This is a great experience which fills him with hope and joy. Here he is:

(*By kind permission of Kobori Nanrei, Daitokuji, Kyoto*)

This is the invitation. This is the call. He did not put those footprints there by his own efforts. He found them. Perhaps he had been looking at them every day for some time; but now he sees them with his inner eye. They are a gift. They are grace.

And his life changes. Powerfully motivated, he is determined to follow those tracks even if it costs him his life. He will follow and his eye of love will see that ox (what an enlightenment!) which symbolizes true wisdom.

The remaining pictures describe his journey with its conflicts and sufferings and surprises. This need not concern us just now. Only let me say that the man is archetypal: he represents the mystic.[1]

---

[1] For other pictures see Johnston (3), pp. 80–1.

Indeed this man following those tracks is not unlike that other man who caught a glimpse of the treasure hidden in the field and with great joy gave up everything (and everything means everything) to buy that field. Or like the man who sold everything to buy the pearl of great price. He is not unlike our father Abraham who went out from his kindred and his father's house to a land that he did not know. In his tremendous sacrifices that man is even like those of whom it is written: 'They were stoned, they were sawn in two, they were killed with the sword; they went about in skins of sheep and goats, destitute, afflicted, ill-treated – of whom the world was not worthy – wandering over deserts and mountains, and in dens and caves of the earth' (Hebrews 11:37,38).

For the vital question is: What motivated that man? What was burning in his heart?

I have said that it was the living flame of love or the blind stirring of love or unrestricted love. But now I would like to put it in theological language and call it *faith*. Mysticism is a journey of faith – deep, dynamic, awe-inspiring, naked faith. Zen constantly speaks of 'great faith' without much clarity about the object of this faith; and Pure Land Buddhism talks always of faith. This flame of faith, this infrastructure in religious experience, is found everywhere and the path along which it leads is always similar. Of course the superstructure of belief is very different. Indeed, a great Chinese commentator on these pictures observes that the man caught sight of the footprints *while reading the sutras*. A Christian, on the other hand, might well see the footprints *while reading the Gospel*. But nevertheless one can scarcely deny that the powerful Buddhist faith which drove that man to search for the ox, and the unshakable Jewish faith which burned in the heart of Abraham when he left his country, and the joyful Christian faith which impelled the man to buy the field in which lay the hidden treasure – that all these have something in common. This is what I call the infrastructure where the mystics of all religions meet, where they recognize one another and feel united.[1]

---

[1] Let me again emphasize that I am not saying that the superstructure is unimportant or that any superstructure will do. The same God who speaks to the heart speaks through the superstructure in history. I am stressing that what all the mystics have in common is the grace or inner gift of the same God.

II

The oxherding pictures are highly symbolical. Now let me try to say more practically how men and women enter into the mystical life.

There are in fact many paths and I have spoken about them else-where (Johnston (3), ch. 5). Here let me select another which developed within Eastern Orthodox Christianity and is now popular throughout the world. This is the beautiful Jesus prayer wherein one recites the formula: 'Lord Jesus Christ, Son of God, have mercy on me a sinner'; or just the name 'Jesus'; or 'It is the Lord' (John 21:7), or one of the several variations. In Japanese one version is the word *Shu* meaning Lord or Kyrios; and some Japanese Christians sit in the lotus and repeat this word with the exhalation of the breath: *Shuuuuu*. In this way it resembles the use of *mu*, meaning nothing, which is used frequently in Zen. It need not, however, be recited with the breathing and some people prefer to repeat the word natur-ally in accordance with their own body-and-spirit rhythm. In fact, this prayer seems to arise spontaneously, without help or direction from a teacher, in Christian hearts throughout the world. What is important is the name – it is precisely here that the power resides – and it is claimed that this prayer goes back to New Testament times and even, in a sense, to the Old Testament where there was profound reverence for the name of God.

It should be noted that the prayer must be recited with faith in Jesus who is Lord. This is of the utmost importance. For in the modern world we hear of the mantra or sound constantly repeated to deepen awareness. One simply recites a meaningless sound or counts the breathing – 'one, two, three' – to clear the upper layers of consciousness in order that the deeper forces of the psyche may be brought into play. Now the Jesus prayer may have something in common with this in that it also empties the upper layers of con-sciousness to allow the deeper forces to work; but it is not only this. Incomparably more important is the faith of which it is an ex-pression. This faith is not only in the Jesus who lives in my heart but also the Jesus who lives in the whole universe, especially in the poor and suffering and afflicted. Consequently, one who truly recites this prayer with faith is never locked up in his little ego but is opened up to a unity with Jesus who is Lord of all.

At first the prayer may be recited aloud like any vocal prayer: it may be formulated with the lips or harmonized with the breathing. On the other hand, it may also be recited interiorly. But in either case it may initially demand effort and perseverance. As time goes on, however, it becomes interiorized to such an extent that it acquires its own rhythm within us. Theophane the Recluse[1] writes charmingly that after the initial effort the prayer becomes like a brook that murmurs in the heart: 'At first this saving prayer is usually a matter of strenuous effort and hard work. But if one concentrates on it with zeal it will begin to flow of its own accord like a brook that murmurs in the heart. This is a great blessing; and it is worth working hard to obtain it' (Ware, p. 117). On and on goes the Jesus prayer of its own accord and without effort on our part, even in the midst of work and activity. 'The prayer takes a firm and steadfast hold when a small fire begins to burn in the heart. Try not to quench this fire, and it will become established in such a way that the prayer repeats itself; and then you will have within you a small murmuring stream' (Kadloubovsky and Palmer, p. 110).

The small murmuring stream! It continues to flow in the depth of one's being, altering one's whole countenance, dominating one's whole person so that every word and action spring only from it. Its rhythm may identify with the beating of the heart, becoming an endless source of joy and gratitude and inner freedom. 'And I live, now not I; but Christ lives in me' (Galatians 2:20). Through the Jesus prayer man is divinized becoming another Christ. He comes to the 'prayer without ceasing' (Luke 18:1) which was the ideal of the famous Russian pilgrim and is now the ideal of thousands of men and women who believe.

A similar pattern is found in Pure Land Buddhism where one recites the name of Amida with faith and trust in his infinite compassion and love. For Amida, teaches Pure Land Buddhism, has made a vow to save all those who take refuge in him and call upon his name.[2] After some time believers find that the name repeats itself. It is no longer 'I' who call upon the name of Amida: the name is reciting itself within me. And there exist today believers in Pure Land Buddhism whose hearts are filled with boundless trust in Amida – his sacred name is always on their lips with gratitude and

---

[1] Theophane the Recluse (1815-94) was an Orthodox bishop who translated the *Philokalia* from Greek into Russian.

[2] The formula used in Japanese is *Namu Amida Butsu* meaning 'I take refuge in the Buddha Amida' or 'Adoration to the Buddha Amida'. This is called the *nembutsu*.

joy. Most of them are simple people who have never heard the word mysticism nor its Japanese equivalent; but the small fire and the murmuring stream live within them.

In this process one abandons thinking and reasoning. The recitation of the sacred name brushes aside all thoughts and one enters a cloud of unknowing. 'When you notice thoughts arising and accosting you,' writes the *Philokalia*, 'do not look at them even if they are not bad; but keeping the mind firmly in the heart, call to Lord Jesus and you will soon sweep away the thoughts and drive out their instigators – the demons – invincibly scorching and flogging them with the Divine name' (Kadloubovsky and Palmer, p. 81).[1] And in this way one comes to the sacred emptiness and detachment from thinking which characterizes the mystical state. There may come a time when even the word Jesus is no longer necessary because a total unitive silence reigns in the heart; and here again one is in nakedness and darkness with no other light than that which burns in one's heart.

III

I have used many words to describe mystical experience which in the end is ineffable. I have used all kinds of symbols. I have called it a small flame of love, a determination to follow the ox, an infinite trust in Amida. But perhaps in the last analysis it is best described as a being in love. For being in love is different from plain loving. I may love many people; but if I am in love with a woman the thought of my loved one is always in my mind and heart like the small fire or the murmuring stream. She dwells in me and I in her.

Mysticism is like that; and the mystics are men and women in love, in love without restriction. That is why contemplatives from Origen to Bernard of Clairvaux and on to St John of the Cross have sung passionately about the man who loves the woman and the woman who loves the man. Their erotic language has embarrassed the pious; their interpretations of the Song of Songs have dismayed the exegete; their sexual symbols have intrigued the psychologist. But when all is said and done, is this not a good way to express it? A profound love which consumes the whole person. Earlier in this book I spoke of the secrecy and hidden quality of this mystical love.

[1] See also p. 280: 'Attention is unceasing silence of the heart, free of all thoughts. At all times, constantly and without ceasing, it breathes Christ Jesus the Son of God and God and him alone . . '

I will not deny this now; but let me say that it is not always secret and hidden. It may become all-consuming and surge to a ravishing climax as St John of the Cross declares: 'Because the enkindling of love in the spirit sometimes increases exceedingly, the longing for God becomes so intense that it will seem to a person that his bones are drying up in this thirst, his nature withering away, and his ardour and strength diminishing through the liveliness of the thirst of love. A person will feel that this is a living thirst' (*Dark Night* 1: 11, I 319).

Such a thirst also consumes the psalmist who longs for God as the hart longs for flowing streams. And again he thirsts for the infinite as one in a parched land thirsts for water:

> O God, thou art my God, I seek thee,
> my soul thirsts for thee;
> my flesh faints for thee,
> as in a dry and weary land where no water is
> (Psalm 63)

Such is the cry of the mystic.

I have said that the mystical life begins with an invitation. But it is an invitation which is repeated many times: 'Friend, go up higher' (Luke 14:10). 'If today you hear his voice, harden not your hearts . . .' (Psalm 95).

10. *Journey into the Void*

Once called, the mystic starts out on a journey. And what a journey, this going forth into the desert and into the void!

First of all, it is filled with conflict from the very start. The man who sees the footprints feels called to follow them, but he also wants to stay in the forest. After all he knows the forest; it is familiar territory; it has its crude and sensual joys. Why venture out into the night? And even if he conquers his fears and tears himself away from his clinging to the forest he will find the same conflict at every stage of his journey. He will always have to keep moving on, leaving what is familiar to enter a terrain that is unfamiliar. At times he may get discouraged and decide that he has had enough. 'What a crazy journey! Let me stay in this outhouse at the fringe of the forest . . . But no, I must go on and on and on, always following the call of love which I hear in the distance.'

When I say he leaves the forest, however, do not take me too literally. If he is employed in the bank of Tokyo he may stay in the bank of Tokyo. But then he will make an inner journey into the unknown. He will travel into ever new states of consciousness, passing through successive stages of the psyche and moving towards the ground of being where dwells the great mystery which we call the Spirit of God. And in this process he will be changed, radically changed, in such wise that he will come to think and feel in a new way – and he may see things in a way so different from the other executives in the bank of Tokyo that he finds himself in the midst of conflict and friction once again. Yes, the person who embarks on this journey is asking for trouble; for he may come into conflict not only with executives in the bank of Tokyo but with ecclesiastical authority in his own backyard. This can be a painful affair.

Yet follow the call he must, even when it leads him to leave everything. For on this journey one must travel light, getting rid of superfluous and burdensome paraphernalia. This is precisely what the Lord said to his disciples:

> Take
> no gold,
> nor silver,
> nor copper in your belts,
> no bag for your journey,
> nor two tunics,
> nor sandals,
> nor a staff
> > (Matthew 10:9,10)

In short, take nothing! All your security must rest in faith alone.
Dom Helder Camara puts it well:

> You want to be,
> excuse me,
> First get free
> of that excess
> of goods
> which cram
> your whole body
> leaving no room
> for you and even less
> for God[1]

As I have already indicated, one may not literally leave these things
(just as one need not leave the bank of Tokyo) but one must learn
to live without them; one must leave attachment and clinging. Non-
attachment is here the big word.

This non-attachment could be, and has been, analysed in considerable detail; but here let me just mention two practical points.

The first is: let go of anxieties. This is the message of the Sermon
on the Mount and it is of cardinal importance in the mystical
journey. For amidst all the useless and superfluous baggage the most
useless and superfluous things are fear, anxiety, scrupulosity and the
like. So don't be anxious about your life, what you shall eat, or about
your body what you shall put on. Look at the flowers of the field:
they are not anxious and yet our Father clothes them. Above all,
don't be anxious about the future, for the future will look after
itself. And don't look with anxiety or guilt or nostalgia into your

[1] *The Desert is Fertile* by Dom Helder Camara (Orbis Books, New
York, 1976, p. 23).

romantic past. Let go of those anxieties. They don't help. Live in the present.

Beautiful, you will say. Yes, but how difficult! Because we love our anxieties; we cling to them and, what is more, they are buried deep, deep down in the psyche. That means that we are always being liberated from subliminal anxieties in this great journey. We are constantly liberated from fear. 'Do not be afraid. I will be with you.'

The second practical point is closely related to this and it is this: Surrender all attachment to thinking – that is to say, to discursive thinking, to images and concepts and knowledge of any kind. (But let me again stress that one does not give up knowledge: one gives up attachment to knowledge.) And this is difficult because, as wise Aristotle says at the beginning of the *Metaphysics*, man naturally desires to know and to use his rational faculties. But it is only by abandoning rational knowledge that one can enter into the silence of faith and the night of supraconceptuality – it is only in this way that one can move towards the ray of darkness about which Dionysius speaks so eloquently.

And yet renunciation of discursive thinking is only the first step. One must not cling to the joys of mystical silence or the rapture of enlightenment or the consolations of passive love. One must cling *to nothing*: this is the void. One must not even cling to noble thoughts and feelings about God, for these thoughts and feelings are not God. If you wish, you may cling to God as He is in Himself. But this is not very helpful because in this life God is the void, God is the nothingness, God is the cloud of unknowing. He is fullness and everything and wisdom in Himself; but He is like nothingness and emptiness and the cloud to us. For no man ever sees God.

Renunciation of clinging is the negative aspect. But let us not forget the positive. Let us recall that this man is led and drawn by the power of love that burns in his heart and the pillar of fire that goes ahead. And it is precisely this love that makes him relinquish all. His love makes him detached. And it is precisely his love which renders him joyful in his nudity of spirit: he can throw everything away with great *élan* – with a smile and a song.

And so the journey is one of great insecurity and of great security. It is desperately insecure because he has no money nor copper (and which of us does not like to rattle the money in our pocket?) to give him human security; it is secure in that he relies on faith. 'No other light to guide me than that which burns in my heart.'

For as he journeys along, a great love is welling up within him and he is being transformed by the fire of love that burns in his breast.

Let me attempt to explain this phenomenon in terms of the non-action or *wu-wei* which is central to Asian thinking.

II

It is principally in Taoism that we hear of non-action. We are told that there are two aspects of human conduct and human growth: *the way of conscious effort* and *the way of non-action*. The way of conscious effort is particularly important in the first part of life and in the pre-mystical stage. Quite simply it is the way of the person who thinks, asks questions, deliberates, weighs the evidence and makes decisions. And if such a person happens to be a politician or a big businessman or a leader of some kind then his decisions may build or destroy the lives of millions of people. But more than that: they will build or destroy his own life. For through his decisions he creates his character and makes himself.

But there is another way: that of non-action and this pertains usually (but by no means exclusively) to the second part of life. Here I am less preoccupied with doing things and more able to let things happen, less intent on making decisions and more able to allow the true decision to well up from the depths of my being. 'Truly, truly I say to you, when you were young you girded yourself and walked where you would; but when you are old, you will stretch out your hands and another will gird you and carry you where you do not wish to go' (John 21:18). These words addressed to Peter might well be addressed to all of us. When we are young, particularly when we are young in the things of the spirit, we walk the path of conscious effort; but when we are mature we are carried along the path of non-action.

Of course, the word non-action is easily misunderstood. For this reason and to avoid misunderstanding, some people prefer to emphasize the active dimension of this process by calling it non-interference or active inaction or creative quietude. Yet others speak of 'doing nothing' and this is all right provided we remember that while we are doing nothing a deeper force within us is doing something or doing everything. I myself like to speak of the great art of *letting things happen* in one's psyche and in the world. The man of Tao is the one who can let the Tao act (and the Tao is the great unnameable mystery that hovers over human life) without putting any impediment in its way. This means that he can follow his deepest spiritual instincts without breaking the law. Confucius is reported to have said that at seventy he could do anything at the dictates of his heart without violating any rule of conduct. Yes, at the age of seventy – not before!

I have said that this non-action is found all over the East. There is more than a hint of it in Gandhi's non-violence: his belief in the power of suffering and fasting and imprisonment. For underlying this is a conviction that Truth will win out. Gandhi spoke constantly of the force of truth: *satyagraha*.

Again this non-action is found in Zen:

> Sitting, only sitting
> And the grass grows green by itself.

I sit in the lotus and allow the Tao to act: I do not interfere: I believe that the Tao will act benevolently in me and in the whole world.

Again, there is something of the *wu-wei* in transcendental meditation. Here I quietly recite a mantra without understanding its meaning. In this way I bind the discursive intellect in such wise that the deeper powers within me begin to work: these deeper forces are a source of creativity and human potential. More examples could be given. The principle simply is that if we can learn the gentle art of doing nothing, of letting things happen, of not putting obstacles in the way, then the forces of nature will act powerfully and beautifully in the universe and in human life.

III

I have spoken about non-action because it is of cardinal importance in the mystical journey. Beginners, of course, will ordinarily meditate according to the way of conscious effort. That is to say, they will think about the Bible or they will make lengthy prayers to God with fervour and devotion or they will repeat the Jesus prayer with considerable effort and they will make resolutions to do good works; but there comes a time when they must cease from discursive meditation and active effort in order that those realities which lie deeper in the psyche may begin to talk. In other words they must pass from conscious effort to non-action: they must let the Spirit act, they must not put impediments in his way. This means that they pass from action to a non-action, which is paradoxically a new level of even more powerful action.

Practically, this entails the abandonment of reasoning and thinking and of any effort whatsoever. Let things happen! Let the Spirit act! God is a great artist and you are the model. If you keep jumping around, the artist cannot paint a masterpiece. So keep quiet. 'Be still and know that I am God' (Psalm 46:10). Listen to the wise advice of St John of the Cross:

> The attitude necessary . . . is to pay no attention to discursive meditation, since this is not the time for it. They should allow the soul to remain in rest and quietude, even though it may seem very obvious to them that they are doing nothing and wasting time, and even though they think this disinclination to think about anything is due to their laxity. Through patience and perseverance in prayer, they will be doing a great deal without activity on their part. All that is required of them here is freedom of soul, that they liberate themselves from the impediment and fatigue of ideas and thoughts and care not about thinking and meditating. They must be content simply with a loving and peaceful attentiveness to God, and live without concern, without effort, and without the desire to taste or feel Him. All these desires disquiet the soul and distract it from the peaceful quiet and sweet idleness of the contemplation which is being communicated to it.
>
> (*Dark Night* 1:10,4)

How difficult this non-action is for some people! It is particularly difficult for Westerners or for Orientals who have received Western education. They feel that they are being lazy, that they are wasting their time, that they ought to get busy in the way of conscious effort. This is a time when they must somehow learn to understand their own situation – to understand what is happening in their lives. But if at this time they meet an incompetent director (and such directors abound) then they are in trouble.

This state is sometimes called passive, though for reasons which I have stated earlier I am wary about this word. But whatever you call it, it grows. It may even happen that one seems to become more and more helpless. At first one was aware of an obscure sense of presence but eventually even this may go – and one is just listening, waiting, and nothing seems to happen. The whole situation may be painful as one's experience becomes more and more 'secret' and 'hidden'. It is now most of all that the mystics use words like emptiness, darkness, obscurity and the void. Some people object to these negative words; but how else can one describe the experience? Most mystics, East and West, find these words useful. Only one must remember that they are descriptive. The experience itself is far from negative: one has given up walking in order to be carried, carried in the arms of God.

The fact is, let me repeat, that in giving up thinking and reasoning, in letting go of those anxieties I am allowing myself to be loved by God. And isn't that the main thing in life? Not that we love God but that God first loves us. He is taking care of me; he is clothing me and nourishing me just as he nourishes and clothes the birds of the air and the flowers of the field. He is loving me through other people (often their love is His love made incarnate) and why should I struggle against it by my conscious efforts? Why should I obscure it with my anxieties? Why should I fight against this love? Remember the words of Isaiah:

> Woe to him who strives with his maker
> An earthen vessel with the potter
> (Isaiah 45:9)

When in empty faith I am doing nothing, a limitless divine love is welling up within me and taking over my life. The emptiness, the void, the darkness – this is infinite love dwelling in the depths of my being. The important thing is that I surrender to this love and allow it to envelop my life.

But this is not easy. Even Paul fought and struggled and kicked against the goad. The problem was that he did not recognize love when he saw it. And so he fights and begs to be delivered from the sting of the flesh that torments him, until the answer comes: 'My grace is sufficient for you for my power is made perfect in weakness' (2 Corinthians 12:9). It is precisely when we are beaten down and helpless and weak that the deepest power within us, the real Tao of endless love, rises to the surface. Paul now understands this. Overflowing with joy he cries out:

> For the sake of Christ, then,
> I am content with weaknesses, insults,
> hardships, persecutions and calamities;
> for when I am weak, then I am strong.
> (2 Corinthians 12:10)

Yes. When Paul is weak the power of Jesus begins to act in him. And this has been true of so many people. It was precisely when their health collapsed and their work failed and their reputation was sullied – it was precisely then that the power and the glory and the love of God surfaced in their lives. This point is beautifully worked out by Graham Greene in *The Power and the Glory*. When I am weak, then I am strong. Something analogous appears in the mission of the disciples to which I have already referred. It is precisely when they have no gold or silver or copper in their purse, when they are rejected by men and dragged before governors and kings, when they give up reasoning and thinking and anxiety about what they will say – it is precisely then that the Spirit rises up and speaks within them – 'for what you are to say will be given to you in that hour; for it is not you who speak, but the Spirit of your Father speaking through you' (Matthew 10:19,20). Here non-action reaches a powerful climax of supreme action.

IV

I have tried to describe the journey. And what a journey! It is the journey of one who is in love without reservation or restriction, who has an endless thirst, whose love goes on and on and on and on as he searches for the ox or crosses the desert. It is a journey that has its conflicts, its failures, its disappointments, its compromises, its temptations, its neuroses – for this unrestricted love (as I have already pointed out) is not perfect love even though it is the most human of human loves.

But in this path, I have tried to say, it is much more important to receive love than to love, much more important to be loved than to love. This is *wu-wei* in a mystical setting. It is the situation of one who tries to drop his defences and his clinging and his selfishness so that this immense love may inundate his whole person and take over his life. And when this happens the love with which he loves others is not his own but the divine love which is a gift. Only such love can go out to one's enemies as to one's friends, only such love can go sincerely and authentically to the poor, the sick, the underprivileged and the imprisoned.

Of course we fight against love. And no wonder. Because it transforms us, changes us into another person – and we don't like to be changed: we like to stay where we are. Because to be changed is to die and rise. This love, says St John of the Cross, kills in order to give life:

> In killing You changed death to life
> (*Living Flame*, Stanza 2)

But in what way does it change us?

The Christian tradition, beginning with Paul and John, tells us that we die to ourselves in order to live to Christ. 'Truly, truly, I say to you, unless a grain of wheat falls into the earth and dies, it remains alone; but if it dies, it bears much fruit. He who loves his life loses it, and he who hates his life in this world will keep it for eternal life' (John 12:24,25). And so we lose our own centre to fall into that deeper centre which is the Word of God living in us. When this happens we can say with Paul: 'It is no longer I who live but Christ who lives in me . . .' (Galatians 2:20). Christian mysticism is a transformation into Christ.

Obviously Buddhists would not accept this Christian interpretation of mystical experience. Yet for them too, I believe, there is a death and a resurrection. Let us remember that that mythical man who searches for the ox finally loses himself completely. No man and no ox remain. Just the big circle of nothingness.

But the big circle is not the end. The man comes to life again. Transformed and enlightened, the compassionate old sage returns to the market-place to save all sentient beings. Now his love is a new love and he is a new man – a new creation. Something has died and something new has been born.

11. *Oriental Nothingness*

The words 'nothingness' and 'emptiness' are constantly on the lips of Oriental mystics. In some sects of Buddhism it is even said that whoever grasps 'nothing' or *mu* has reached the heart of the matter and is already enlightened. The distinguished Japanese philosopher Yoshinori Takeuchi goes so far as to say that nothingness or non-being is the very foundation of Oriental philosophy and religion whereas Western thought is based upon being. Here are his words:

> Whenever discussion arises, concerning the problem of encounter between being and non-being, Western philosophers and theologians, with hardly an exception, will be found to align themselves on the side of being. This is no wonder. The idea of 'being' is the Archimedean point of Western thought. Not only philosophy and theology but the whole tradition of Western civilization have turned around this pivot. All is different in Eastern thought and Buddhism. The central notion from which Oriental religious intuition and belief as well as philosophical thought have been developed is the idea of 'nothingness'. To avoid serious confusion, however, it must be noted that East and West understand non-being or nothingness in entirely different ways. (Waldenfels)

Now it is sometimes said that few Orientals and no Occidentals understand Oriental nothingness. Probably, however, this is an exaggeration. There are some Occidentals who have spent years or decades in assiduous Buddhist training and discipline and who undoubtedly have achieved insight into the mystery of *mu*. But I myself do not claim to be one of them. Consequently, I can do little more than introduce my reader to some of the basic problems of *mu* and then move on to nothingness in the Western mystical tradition which is more properly my field. I hope that some day we will receive an explanation of Oriental nothingness from the pen of an enlightened Buddhist who will at the same time direct his inner eye to the corresponding problem in the West.

II

The *Upanishads* speak of many different layers of consciousness, the deepest of which is compared to a deep and dreamless sleep in which the mind is swept clean of all images and thoughts and subject-object relationships. This, an intense form of that pure or un-differentiated consciousness about which I spoke earlier in this book, has always been associated with the Sanskrit word *sunyata* which is generally translated as 'emptiness' or 'voidness' or 'nothingness'. Yet *sunyata* never means the death of all things or absolute negation: it has a positive connotation.

In the Buddhist wisdom literature composed in India between 100 BC and AD 600 the word *sunyata* continues to be of cardinal importance. Later it is brought to China and translated into Chinese by two vibrant characters which today are splendidly inscribed over the gates of Buddhist temples throughout Japan. The first character, pronounced *mu* in Japanese and *wu* in Chinese and translated into English as *nothing* is:

(*By kind permission of Kakichi Kadowaki*)

If you ask a Zen master to draw a character which expresses his deepest insight, it is more than likely that he will take up his brush and draw *mu*. This will be his parting gift as you leave the temple.

The second character is pronounced *ku* and is usually translated as *emptiness:*

(*By kind permission of Kakichi Kadowaki*)

This same character is also used for the sky: the great emptiness of the vault of heaven which resembles *sunyata*.

Now while these two characters and the ideas for which they stand sound disturbingly negative to Western ears, any authentic Buddhist will insist that they contain a very positive dimension.[1] That is why Takeuchi can say that the Eastern understanding of these words is quite different from that of the West and that 'the

---

[1] A standard Japanese Buddhist dictionary renders *ku* as sunyata: '*Sunyata* does not deny the concept of existence as such . . . it must not be confused with nihilism or a denial of the existence of phenomena in any form' (*Japanese-Buddhist Dictionary*, Daito Shuppansha, Tokyo, 1965).

absolute must be considered first as Absolute Nothingness' (Waldenfels).

On a more popular level, when Queen Elizabeth of Britain was visiting Japan, she was brought to a Zen temple over which the great character *mu* was inscribed. 'What does that mean?' she asked the Buddhist monk who guided her. 'That means God' he answered. No doubt he felt that such an answer while not completely accurate or satisfactory was least open to misunderstanding.

But let me first refer to two aspects of *mu* which are less difficult to grasp.

The first I call cultural nothingness because it has penetrated Sino-Japanese culture in a remarkable way and is known to any educated person who lives in East Asia. It is found in the concept of no-mind (*mu-shin*) or non-self (*mu-ga*) which is central to the practice of the tea-ceremony, the flower arrangement and calligraphy as well as to the martial arts like fencing, judo and karate. It is closely associated with the Taoist non-action (*wu-wei*) about which I spoke in the last chapter and is the mental state of one who submerges his ego or little self in order that the forces of life may begin to work within. The mind is emptied of reasoning and thinking, of all sense of subject and object, in order that the life-force which is centred in the belly may rise up – and it does rise up, giving extraordinary power to the person who has mastered this art of non-self or no-mind.

Yet non-self can be religious as well as cultural. At a temple near Tokyo famous for its great statue of the Bodhisattva Kannon, one can read the inscription: 'The person of non-self (*mu-ga no hito*) can see with the inner eye.' While the self remains, enlightenment will not come. It is when the illusory self dies that the real self is born and the inner eye awakens and comes to see.

A second aspect of *mu* which is central to Buddhist practice is the *ascetical mu*. That is to say the non-attachment, the abandonment of clinging and craving and inordinate desire. Repeating the word *mu* one drops all that superfluous baggage about which I have spoken, thus attaining to inner liberty and poverty of spirit. This again has Taoist influence and is based on the notion that when one abandons clinging, the Tao will act within.

As I have said, the cultural and ascetical aspects of *mu* are not difficult to understand. Much more mysterious and problematic is the ontological or metaphysical *mu* on which the others are built. For *mu* is regarded as an absolute and as perfect wisdom.

III

In the thirty-eight books which compose the *Prajnaparamita*, literature pride of place is given to the *Heart Sutra* of the perfection of wisdom, which claims to formulate the heart or essence or core of perfect wisdom and to put into words (impossible task) the experience of nirvana and of *sunyata*. In Chinese this sutra consists of only two hundred and sixty-two words which can be printed on a single page; and it is recited constantly in Zen temples. With something like awe I have attended the early morning liturgy at *Eiheiji*, the central temple of the Soto sect, watching a hundred monks, clad in Buddhist robes, march rhythmically to and fro to the sound of the gong while reciting the *Heart Sutra*. Although no translation will bring out the melody of those Chinese sounds, I would like to quote some of the sentences in English. The Sutra begins:

> When the Bodhisattva Avalokitesvara was in deep meditation of *prajnaparamita* (transcendental wisdom) he saw that all the five skandhas are empty; thus he overcame all suffering and ills.

Here the important word is 'saw'. The Bodhisattva, without the aid of discursive reasoning, got a direct intuition into the total emptiness of all things including the five skandhas.[1] And precisely through this enlightenment he was liberated from suffering and ill. This again is a notion that is deeply rooted in Buddhism: that through transcendental wisdom we are saved and liberated.

The sutra goes on to speak of emptiness, of *sunyata*. It does so in radically negative terms:

> All that has its own characteristic or form . . . is empty of the form: no arising, no ceasing; no contamination, no lack of contamination; no increase, no decrease. Therefore, in emptiness is no physical component, no sensation, no representation, no will, no consciousness; no eye, no ear, no nose, no tongue, no body, no mind; no shape, no colour, no sound, no smell, no taste, no touch, no concept; no visible world . . . no consciously perceivable world;

[1] According to Buddhist philosophy man consists of five heaps or layers known as *skandhas*. They are: the body, feelings, perceptions, impulses and emotions, acts of consciousness. These five heaps are everything in man and the ego is illusory.

no ultimate ignorance, no extinction of ultimate ignorance, no ageing and dying; no suffering, no cause of suffering, no extinction of suffering, no practice which leads to the extinction of suffering; no knowing, no attainment, no non-attainment.

This array of negatives is a hymn in praise of *sunyata* or *ku* or nirvana. The same idea can be expressed pictorially by the great circle of nothingness or zero which is so characteristic of Zen art. It is the picture which we see when the ox has disappeared, the man has disappeared and only the voice cries out: 'Not a thing is! Nothing!':

One way to approach nothingness is through the *koan* practice in Zen.[1] Sitting in the lotus with back straight and eyes slightly open,

[1] *Koan* One way of practising Zen in the Rinzai sect is to keep before the mind's eye a riddle or enigmatic problem or *koan* which cannot be solved by discursive reasoning.

one simply repeats the word *mu* with the breathing. One repeats it again and again and again for hours, for days, for weeks, until eventually one comes to *realize mu* and to identify with it. This is a great enlightenment. Moreover, it is ongoing: one can get more and more insight into *mu*: there is no end to its treasures. The Master will ask questions to probe the depth of one's realization: 'What is *mu*? Show me *mu*. What size is *mu*? What shape? What colour?' There is no fixed answer to these questions but an experienced master knows with unerring intuition whether or not the response comes from an enlightened consciousness. He can sense at once whether the student has become one with *mu* or is still separated from it.

In Zen, *mu* is called 'the barrier without gates'. One must strive with might and main to break through this great barrier which leads from the phenomenal world into the world of enlightenment. But one does not understand *mu* with the rational intellect. Here is a famous description of the approach:

Now, tell me, what is the barrier of the Zen Masters? Just this *mu* – it is the barrier of Zen. It is thus called 'the gateless barrier of Zen'. Those who have passed the barrier will not only see Joshu clearly, but will go hand in hand with all the Masters of the past, see them face to face. You will see with the same eye that they see with and hear with the same ear. Wouldn't it be wonderful? Don't you want to pass the barrier? Then concentrate yourself into this *mu*, with your 360 bones and 84,000 pores, making your whole body one great inquiry. Day and night work intently at it. Do not attempt nihilistic or dualistic interpretations. It is like having bolted a red-hot iron ball. You try to vomit it but cannot. Cast away your illusory discriminating knowledge and consciousness accumulated up to now, and keep on working harder. After a while, when your efforts come to fruition, all the oppositions (such as in and out) will naturally be identified. You will then be like a dumb person who has had a wonderful dream: he only knows it personally, within himself. Suddenly you break through the barrier; you will astonish heaven and shake the earth.

(Shibayama, p. 19)

In this way one becomes *mu*.

'What is *mu*?' asks the Master. 'I am *mu*,' answers the disciple. 'Show me *mu*,' says the Master. 'You are looking at *mu*,' retorts the disciple instantaneously. '*Mu* walked in through that door. *Mu* is talking to you.' But this is only the beginning. There is no end to *mu*.

IV

Confronted with the mystery of Oriental nothingness, Western philosophers have frequently used words like nihilistic, life-denying, pessimistic. Some have not hesitated to call Buddhism atheistic. I believe (and I have already quoted Buddhists to support me) that this is a misunderstanding: we must not blind ourselves to the extremely positive elements which lie behind the negative language.

First of all we must remember that Buddhism is above all a religion of salvation. It claims to save man from the illusions and snares and suffering of human existence. The four noble truths which are the basis of all forms of Buddhism declare that existence is suffering but then hasten to add that *there is a way out:* man's situation is not hopeless: there is light beyond the darkness. Is not this a positive dimension?

Moreover, the way out is through enlightenment or a series of enlightenments culminating in the supreme experience of nirvana. Far from being negative, enlightenment is an experience of joy, liberation and release from anxiety. The *Heart Sutra* which I have quoted speaks of the fearlessness and joy of the man who has realized and attained to the perfection of wisdom. It is paralleled in all the mystical traditions where there comes a time when one is liberated from fear and says with Julian of Norwich, 'All will be well, and all will be well, and all manner of things will be well.' All may not look well. It may look all wrong. But deep down in my heart I have a security and a certainty that everything is all right.

Again, let us remember that while the oxherding pictures originally ended with the great circle of *mu*, two pictures were subsequently added which are positive and deeply significant.

The first is called 'the return to the source'. It tells the myth of the eternal return. If you go on a journey you return to your starting point – like Chesterton's adventurous man who set sail from Plymouth on a journey of discovery and found England, or like the traveller in outer space who turns full circle and comes back to earth, or like all of us who return to the womb: to the womb of the earth. In the same way, the man who went in search of the ox, when the turmoil and conflict and ecstasy is over, returns to himself: he becomes his true self. Just himself, very ordinary, nothing special. Once again, trees are trees, rivers are rivers, valleys are valleys.

But in the last picture he goes one step further and returns to the market-place with great compassion to save all sentient beings. In other words he returns to action.

Now I believe that this compassion which fills his heart is connected with the *mu* and emptiness. For there is an old Buddhist saying that emptiness equals compassion (*ku soku jihi*). This is an emptiness which is akin to what the old Christian writers called humility. When I am humbly and totally empty I can receive others into my heart; when self is forgotten I have room for all men and for God.

There are good reasons, then, for concluding that while all expressions about the ultimate reality in Buddhism are negative that reality itself is positive and that Buddhism is by no means atheistic. There are indeed some Buddhist texts which point to such an interpretation. In the *Pali Canon* of Hinayana Buddhism we read: 'Monks, there is a not-born, a not-become, a not-made, a not-compounded. Monks, if that unborn, not-become, not-made, not-compounded were not, there would be apparent no escape from this here that is born, become, made, compounded. But since, monks, there is an unborn . . . therefore the escape from this here is born' (*Udana*, 80, 81. See Woodward, p. 98). In other words the very fact that there is salvation or deliverance points to the existence of an ultimate reality. We can only speak about it, however, in negative terms.

Yet when all is said and done, even the most enlightened among the enlightened does not grasp Oriental nothingness fully: anyone who claims to have plumbed the depths of *mu*, far from being wise, is a fool. For nothingness is truly a mystery, a mystery in the strictest sense of the word. And this in itself is deeply significant. Because, as I have repeatedly said, all the great religions point to a mystery which hovers over human life yet lies beyond a cloud of unknowing. It is precisely this sense of mystery and of the ineffable that we all have in common. If no one understands nothingness, neither does anyone truly understand God. No one understands Yahweh nor the Tao nor Brahman nor Atman. We are all reduced to silence in the face of mystery. We are all aware that we do not know.

12. *Christian Nothingness*

The apophatic mystics of the West, like their brethren in the East, are lavish in their use of words like nothingness, emptiness, darkness, obscurity and the cloud. Indeed, so dark and negative is their manner of speech that not a few fervent Christians have raised voices of protest. In an excellent book written in the early part of this century and entitled *Western Mysticism*, Dom Cuthbert Butler treats of contemplation in three great mystics of the West: Augustine, Gregory and Bernard of Clairvaux. In extolling enthusiastically the affirmative and deeply Christian dimension of these great giants of the mystical life, Cuthbert Butler shows himself a little uneasy about the nothingness and darkness and secrecy and unknowing of the Dionysian tradition. 'The mystics,' he writes, 'heap up terms of negation – darkness, void, nothingness – in endeavouring to describe the Absolute which they have apprehended. It may be, of course, that their apprehension had such a fullness and richness of content that in human language it could only be described negatively. But one may at least point out that their method is the very opposite of the characteristically Christian one of affirmation; that where they say "darkness" St John says "light", and that St John says "fullness" where they say "void" and St Paul stresses not ignorance but enhanced knowledge, as the result of religious experience' (Butler, p. 179).

These words are representative of a number of deeply Christian contemplatives who react vigorously against the 'neoplatonic contamination' which has infected the springs of Christian mysticism. They will agree that the Rhineland mystics had profound religious experience, but they are wary about the language in which this religious experience is expressed. They will agree that St John of the Cross was a great mystic, a great poet and a great saint – but they are less than happy with his negative theology. Most of all they are wary of an emptiness or nothingness that would negate the value and beauty of God's creation. Some distinguished Christian writers have labelled St John of the Cross Buddhist; and while this might sound complimentary to our modern ecumenical ears it was far from flattering in its original context.

This reaction against the negativity of the Dionysian mystics is even more pronounced today since we live in a culture which has the greatest esteem for human values, human feeling, human sexuality. Ours is a culture which delights in the saying of Irenaeus that the glory of God is man fully alive. It is a culture which believes with Teilhard in the spiritual power of matter. It is a culture which looks with dismay on nothingness and emptiness.

And yet, in spite of all this, we still must ask if there is an authentic Christian *mu* or nothingness. Apart from other considerations, we owe this to the dialogue with our Buddhist brothers and sisters in the East.

II

At a Zen-Christian dialogue which I once attended in Kyoto one of the participants, a Japanese Christian who practises Zen with a small community in the Japanese Alps, was asked to explain his Zen. He rose to his feet and said quite simply: 'The first thing is sincerity . . . My Zen is expressed in the words of Jesus on the Cross: "My God, my God, why hast thou forsaken me?".' A Buddhist participant who was sitting beside me whispered under his breath: 'Beautiful, beautiful!'.

'My God, my God, why has thou forsaken me?' (Matthew 27:46). When Jesus uttered these words he had nothing, absolutely nothing. Previously he had said that his disciples would all be scattered and that they would leave him alone – 'yet I am not alone, for the Father is with me' (John 16:32). But now even the Father has forsaken him and Jesus is left in the void of nothingness and in the dark night of the soul.

These words are, of course, the opening lines of the Twenty-Second Psalm, and some scripture scholars hold that Jesus on the Cross recited the whole psalm or, at least, that the sentiments of the whole psalm were in his mind as he was dying. This is profoundly significant. Because Psalm 22 is messianic – it is a cry of trust in the God who has protected our fathers and has drawn me from the womb of my mother. It ends with a cry of joy and of hope and of triumph:

> All the ends of the earth shall remember
> and turn to the Lord;

> and all the families of the nations
> shall worship before him
>
> (Psalm 22:27)

This is the cry of resurrection. The realization that in the total loss is the total gain. In the nothingness is the everything. In the death is the victory. 'Truly, truly, I say to you, unless a grain of wheat falls into the earth and dies, it remains alone; but if it dies, it bears much fruit' (John 12:24).

Another example of nothingness is found in the Epistle to the Philippians where Paul speaks of the *kenosis* or self-emptying of Jesus – 'who though he was in the form of God, did not count equality with God a thing to be grasped, but emptied himself, taking the form of a servant, being born in the likeness of men' (Philippians 2:6,7). Jesus emptied himself; and it is interesting to note that the Japanese Bible translates this as 'Jesus became *mu*' (*mu to sareta*): Jesus became nothing. But he became even more than nothing because 'being found in human form he humbled himself and became obedient unto death, even death on a cross' (Philippians 2:8). But there can be an even greater humiliation than this, and in another remarkable text Paul says that Jesus became sin: 'For our sake he made him to be sin who knew no sin, so that in him we might become the righteousness of God' (2 Corinthians 5:21). Such was the humiliation, the emptiness, the nothingness of the Son of God. It is beyond words to describe.

But his emptiness is a way to fullness; his nothingness is a way to everything; his humiliation is a way to glory:

> Therefore God has highly exalted him
> and bestowed on him the name which is
> above every name, that at the name of
> Jesus every knee should bow, in heaven
> and on earth and under the earth, and
> every tongue confess that Jesus Christ
> is Lord, to the glory of God the Father
>
> (Philippians 2:9-11)

Here is the resurrection, hailed by every tongue with that formula which in the New Testament is the profession of faith: 'Jesus Christ is Lord'.

All this may seem a thousand miles away from Oriental nothingness. Yet I have heard of a Zen Master who, on reading this passage
from Philippians, nodded his head and said: 'St Paul really understood *mu!*'.

Early in this book I spoke of the mystical experience of Jesus and I
said that it was primarily Trinitarian. Now let me add another very
obvious aspect of this experience: death and resurrection. The
supreme mystical experience of Jesus entailed a total annihilation as
a prelude to an endless glorification. And, moreover, this suffering
and emptiness and death *was necessary*. 'Was it not necessary that
Christ should suffer these things and enter into his glory?' (Luke
24:26).

Now I have also said that the Christian mystical experience is that
of 'another Christ' – as Jesus became nothing in order to be glorified,
so the Christian mystical life is a becoming nothing in order to be
glorified by resurrection. But this pattern is not only Christian. It is
found before the time of Jesus in Abraham who loses everything,
absolutely everything, in order to become the father of a great
nation. The story is told in Genesis and I have referred to it already
in this book. Abraham is about to slay his beloved son thus crushing
all hopes that the promise will be fulfilled, but his hand is stopped
by the angel of the Lord:

> By myself I have sworn, says the Lord,
> because you have done this, and have
> not withheld your son, your only son, I
> will indeed bless you, and I will multiply
> your descendants as the stars of heaven
> and as the sand which is on the seashore.
> And your descendants shall possess the gate of
> their enemies, and by your descendants shall
> all the nations of the earth bless themselves . . .
> (Genesis 22:15–18)

Here Abraham dies; he becomes nothing in order to rise joyfully to
the fulfilment of the promise.

I believe that this pattern of death and resurrection, of nothing and
everything, of emptiness and fullness – this basic pattern is found in
the big enlightenments or mystical experiences of all the great
religions. In Buddhism it is said that there must come a 'great death'

prior to the awakening. Moreover, it is interesting to observe that when Zen masters speak to Christians they frequently use the example of the death and resurrection of Jesus, telling us that like Jesus we must die in order to be reborn. This is because they know from experience that death and resurrection are the warp and woof of human life and they see that Jesus is the archetypal man.

From all this I draw the conclusion that the Cross is the Christian *mu* and the Christian *koan*. Just as *mu* cannot be penetrated by reasoning and thinking, so also the cross is impervious to the rational intellect. But he who understands is flooded with unutterable joy and true wisdom – 'we preach Christ crucified, a stumbling block to Jews and folly to gentiles, but to those who are called, both Jews and Greeks, Christ the power of God and the wisdom of God' (1 Corinthians 1:23,24). These are not mere words. Paul gloried in the cross of Our Lord Jesus Christ by which he was crucified to the world and the world to him; and many Christian mystics through the centuries have had the same foolish enlightenment. Their lives have changed radically when they came to understand, and then to love, the cross. This is something one cannot explain: it is folly and it is a stumbling block.

III

I believe, then, that the *kenosis* or self-emptying of Jesus is the basis and the inspiration for any Christian emptiness or nothingness or loss of self. And, moreover, I believe that the authentic Christian mystics of the Dionysian tradition thought so also. Those who call St John of the Cross Buddhist may overlook the profound significance of a few of the sentences with which he begins his practical advice for progress in the mystical path:

First, have a habitual desire to imitate Christ in all your deeds by bringing your life into conformity with His. You must then study His life in order to know how to imitate Him and behave in all events as He would.
Second . . . Do this out of love for Jesus Christ. In His life He had no other gratification, nor desired any other, than the fulfilment of His Father's will, which He called His meat and food (John 4:34) (*Ascent*, 1:13,3 and 4).

Similar passages could be quoted from the author of *The Cloud*,

Meister Eckhart, and the other Christian Dionysian mystics. These men were impregnated with the spirit of the Gospel.

Yet, having said this, it is also true that other aspects of their spirituality are culturally conditioned. Just as theology changes according to culture and historical conditions (and what a change we witness today!) so also spirituality must change and be incarnated into each age. Consequently I am not at all certain that the overall approach of the mystics of darkness will appeal to modern men and women. I prefer to see it as one spirituality which was valid for people of a certain time and is valid for people of a certain temperament today. But I understand and respect the feelings of those who say that Eckhart and St John of the Cross are not their cup of tea.

Let me, however, select some aspects of the Western mystical nothingness which are worth discussing and may be of interest to Buddhists in our day.

St John of the Cross stresses the nothingness of the whole created universe. At the beginning of the *Ascent* he writes:

> All the creatures of heaven and earth *are nothing* when compared to God, as Jeremiah points out . . . 'I looked at the earth, and it was empty and nothing; and at the heavens and I saw they had no light' (Jeremiah 4:23). *By saying that he saw an empty earth, he meant that all its creatures were nothing and the earth too was nothing.*

Here is a radical statement of the nothingness of the world and it is followed by an even more radical declaration that 'all the beauty of creatures compared with the infinite Beauty of God is supreme ugliness' (*Ascent*, 4:4,3).

Now in all cultures we find people who have a deep insight into the transiency and nothingness and vanity of all things. I am thinking of Qoheleth or of those modern existentialists who speak of man as being-towards-death, and so on. But the nothingness of St John of the Cross is not like this. It is the realization of one who has had a glimpse of infinite beauty and who says that *by comparison* the rest of the world is supreme ugliness. Such a profoundly enlightened person must be forgiven for his poetic hyperbole. All the mystics are tempted to talk in this way. They talk of the light of the sun and the light of the candle, of the all and the nothing; and did not Thomas say that his writings were like straw?

Furthermore, the Thomistic theology which St John of the Cross studied under the Dominicans at Salamanca had integrated the Dionysian theology of negation and in consequence contained a startling paradox: on the one hand all created things are like God and reflect his glory, but on the other hand they are not like God and do not reflect his glory. For only God exists in the complete sense of the word. Things other than God are being and non-being. Seen from one aspect they are: seen from another aspect they are not.

Now is it possible to get an insight into the non-being or nothingness of all things? I think it is. But such an insight is closely associated with a realization of the allness of God. I believe that something like this exists in Hinduism where we are told that the world is only real and intelligible when seen as rooted in Brahman. Separated from him it is *maya* or illusion or nothingness and the person who sees it cut off from its source lives in *avidya* or ignorance.

IV

I have spoken of the nothingness or non-being of the created universe. But is it possible to speak of the nothingness of God?

St John of the Cross will affirm that God is everything. He is light; He is fullness; He is all: He is the source of being and beauty. In this he would seem to be the very opposite of the absolute nothingness about which Oriental mysticism speaks. But (and here again we come against great paradox) while God is light in Himself, He is *darkness to us*; while He is all in Himself, He is *nothing to us*; while He is fullness in Himself, He is *emptiness to us*. St John of the Cross does not say that God is darkness and emptiness and nothingness; but he does say that the human experience of God is darkness and emptiness and nothingness. For God is like night to the soul.

Nor is this mere theory. In the mystical life one enters into the void, into a cloud of unknowing which seems like nothingness. Indeed, a time may come when the darkness is so extreme that one feels abandoned by God – left high and dry with God absent. But if one waits in emptiness one comes to realize that the void is God: it is not a preparatory stage but the experience of God Himself. And in the moment or period of enlightenment though one may say that God who was absent has returned, more correctly one will exclaim: 'God was present all the time and I did not recognize Him. I thought it was darkness but it was light. I thought it was nothing but it was

all. It is not that the darkness has gone away but that I have come
to love the darkness.' As the light blinds the bat or as excessive light
of the sun blinds the human eye, so the excessive light of God
plunges man into thick darkness.

And God is approached in darkness and emptiness and nothingness simply because He is the mystery of mysteries, far above anything that the human eye can see or the human mind imagine, far
above anything that can be conveyed in words: 'No one has ever seen
God' (John 1:18).

That God is mystery, unknowable, ineffable, unlike anything
made by human hands or seen by human eyes – this is stressed all
through the Old Testament. The Jewish historian Josephus tells the
story of how the Roman Pompey after capturing Jerusalem in 63 BC
strode into the holy of holies with some of his followers and found
there *nothing, absolutely nothing*. This was the Hebrew way of
representing the ineffable nature of Yahweh.[1] As for the apophatic
mystics, beginning with Gregory of Nyssa they constantly appeal to
the example of Moses (to what extent the exegetes would support
them I do not know) who ascended the mountain to meet God in the
cloud of unknowing. For, as is said in Chronicles, 'The Lord has said
that he would dwell in thick darkness' (2 Chronicles 6:1). And the
experience of Moses is one of nothingness and darkness even though
his heart is filled with a burning love. This is the darkness of faith, of
naked faith which lives in the mind when all props are gone.

Some years ago while I was chatting with a Zen Master in Kyoto
about *mu* and nothingness I cited the words of St John of the Cross
which I have quoted earlier in this book that in the mystical life
there is nothing to guide me except the love which burns in my
heart. I then observed that St John of the Cross was less radical
than Zen because he says, 'nothing except . . .' whereas Zen says,
'nothing'. The master smiled and said: 'No. I don't think so. This is

---

[1] Pompey captured Jerusalem in 63 BC after a siege of three months.
Josephus tells us that together with some of his followers he entered
the sanctuary but that in accordance with his piety and virtuous
character he touched nothing. In the innermost recess known as the
holy of holies there was nothing whatever: *ouden holos* (Bellum Jud.
5,5,5). The Roman historian Tacitus also relates that Pompey saw
into the holy of holies. It should be noted that this was the second,
post-exilic temple. In the first temple, the temple of Solomon, the ark
was placed in the holy of holies.

one example of the inadequacy of words. Because "*the love which burns in my heart" is also nothing*'. I immediately saw his point and was amazed at his perceptiveness. The love which burns in my heart is nothing because it is faith, pure faith, naked faith which is dark like night and is experienced as nothingness. Yet it is precisely the night and the nothingness which guide; and so St John of the Cross can sing:

> O guiding night
> O night more lovely than the dawn
> (*Ascent*, Stanza 5)

It is in darkness and nothingness and emptiness that one experiences God. The darkness and the emptiness and the nothingness are guiding and leading me on. But let me add a word: the darkness and the nothingness are not necessarily dismal and bleak and unpleasant and painful as the words themselves might indicate and as some writers have suggested. There are, of course, painful periods; but the nothingness is filled with joy and the night is more lovely than the dawn.

St John of the Cross who was an artist as well as a mystic has left us a sketch of the mystical path which leads to the summit of the mountain. At the very centre of the picture is *nothing* (the Spanish *nada*) and the saint writes:

> nothing, nothing, nothing,
> nothing, nothing, nothing,
> And even on the mountain nothing

Renunciation of all clinging and craving! I have mentioned it already: no gold, no silver, no copper in your belt, no bag for your journey, no two tunics, no sandals, no staff. A similar message is found in *The Cloud of Unknowing* where the author tells us to bury everything, absolutely everything, beneath a cloud of forgetting. All this is somewhat similar to the ascetical *mu* of Oriental mysticism. Only remember that this nothingness is not the renunciation of all things, but, the renunciation of clinging to all things – and it is done in order that I may love these same things truly, as they are in themselves, without projections. Once liberated from self-centred craving one gets everything back and can cry with St John of the Cross:

> Now that I least desire them
> I have them all without desire

I have them all! Nothing is renounced. It is the mystic who really loves life and loves people and loves the cosmos and finds joy in all that is beautiful in the universe. He loves all but is the slave to nothing.

The all-important thing to remember (and here I hope I will be forgiven for repeating myself) is that this journey is the answer to a call and is made under the sweet influence of grace and the gentle guidance of the Spirit. Not one step is made except by the power of the same Spirit. This is the path of one who has seen the footprints of the ox or the treasure hidden in the field and sells everything joyfully to follow the ox or to buy the field. It is the renunciation of one who has heard the voice of the beloved: 'Hark! my beloved is knocking' (Song of Songs 5:2). This is very important, because without the call of grace the whole doctrine of *nothing* becomes harsh, grating, inhuman and dismal.

Furthermore it must be remembered, as I have already said, that this loss of all things is eventually something that happens rather than something that I do. Remember the non-action, the *wu-wei*. I don't need to make violent efforts because the power of love which burns within is gradually and gently detaching me from all things, from all people, so that I may be attached to these same things and these same people in a true and nobler way.

And yet the voice of St John of the Cross does grate upon the ears of sensitive souls:

> To reach satisfaction in all
> desire its possession in nothing
> To come to possess all
> desire the possession of nothing,
> To arrive at being all
> desire to be nothing.
>
> To come to the knowledge of all
> desire the knowledge of nothing
> (*Ascent*, 1:13,11)

And in this *todo y nada* the Spanish mystic is not original. The same theme is sung centuries before in *The Book of Privy Counselling* and in Julian of Norwich where we hear of the 'alling and noughting' (Johnston (2), p. 164).

I myself can never understand this in a purely philosophical or ascetical context. To me it only makes sense in view of the *kenosis* of Jesus about which I have spoken. In such a context it is nonsense which makes sense or, as Paul says, foolishness which is wisdom: 'For the foolishness of God is wiser than men . . .' (1 Corinthians 1:25). That is why I believe that those who call St John of the Cross Buddhist and overlook the Christo-centric dimension of his work miss the whole point. Without Christ his doctrine would scarcely be human.

I have spoken of the journey and the way. But words are always inadequate; and of course there is no way. Abraham 'went out, not knowing where he was to go' (Hebrews 11:8). Abraham had no maps. At the beginning there are guidelines and rules which are always helpful and valuable, but at the summit St John of the Cross can write:

> Here there is no longer any way
> Because for the just man there is no law
> He is a law unto himself

The just man is following his deepest spiritual instincts which tell him of the promptings of the Holy Spirit. He is beyond the law.

In Zen one often hears of a state which is 'beyond good and evil'; and this kind of talk has been offensive to pious ears which have interpreted it as a *carte blanche* for licentiousness. But it is not so. It simply means that the enlightened person is beyond *the law* of good and evil because he is guided by the inner light. He is following the counsel of Jesus not to be anxious about what we should say because the Spirit will tell us: 'It is not you who speak, but the Spirit of your Father speaking through you' (Matthew 10:20).

13. *Journey Towards Union*

I have described the mystical journey in negative terms; but I hope it has become abundantly clear that the journey itself is not negative or life-denying. It is a love-filled journey towards union with the All, a journey which can be described in all kinds of symbols and metaphors and figures of speech. Thomas Aquinas explains it theologically in terms of the Genesis myth. Man and woman created in the state of original justice lived happily in Paradise in harmony within themselves, harmony with one another and harmony with God. But by sin they were cruelly divided, split, scattered. Beguiled by the serpent, expelled from Eden, ashamed of their nakedness, they fell into that sadly divided state to which we their children are now reduced. But mysticism or contemplation is a return to harmonious union: it is a process of reconciliation, of inner unification, of magnificent justification. It is as the author of *The Cloud* (he was greatly influenced by Thomas) strikingly states, a one-ing exercise. That is to say, it makes us one with ourselves, one with the human race, one with the All which is God.

And the unity to which mysticism leads is much richer than the original justice which was lost. For 'the free gift is not like the trespass' (Romans 5:13). The new union, found through the grace of Christ and his gift of faith, is ultimately that union for which Jesus prayed at the Last Supper when he asked the Father 'that they may all be one; even as thou, Father, art in me, and I in thee, that they also may be one in us, so that the world may believe that thou hast sent me' (John 17:21).

As can be readily seen, this explanation situates mysticism at the very centre of the Christian life. The mystical life becomes the Christian life and we can understand how there can be a universal call to mysticism. For everyone is called to this union and reconciliation within himself, with the human race and with God. This is the message of Paul in Ephesians.

When it came to describing the pyschological process by which this union was effected the scholastics made use of the philosophy of Plato and Aristotle as it had been assimilated into the Christian tradition. Here the human soul is described as having faculties called exterior senses, interior senses, memory, understanding and will - while the centre or ground of the soul is the great mystery which we call God. Since these faculties have been dissipated and distorted, they must be purified in order that they may once more be focused on God who is their centre. This purification, achieved through the darkness and dryness and emptiness about which I have spoken, leads to a great harmony. For the purified person has faith in the intellect, hope in the memory and love in the will, while his purified senses give light and warmth to the Beloved who dwells within. Indeed, this whole process is nothing less than a divinization of the person who now becomes another Christ, a son by adoption. The in-dwelling Spirit joins himself to his spirit and cries out: 'Abba, Father!'.

In this book I accept this doctrine but I have preferred to use a different psychology which I consider more relevant for the men and women of our day. This psychology speaks in terms of states or layers of consciousness rather than faculties of the soul. In the mystical life one passes from one layer to the next in an inner or downward journey to the core of the personality where dwells the great mystery called God – God who cannot be known directly, cannot be seen (for no man has ever seen God) and who dwells in thick darkness. This is the never-ending journey which is recogniz-able in the mysticism of all the great religions. It is a journey towards union because the consciousness gradually expands and integrates data from the so-called unconscious while the whole personality is absorbed into the great mystery of God.

II

I have already described the journey as that of the man in search of the ox; but at the risk of some repetition I would like to describe it again with a different set of symbols.

And first of all let me recall that if we are inwardly divided this is partly because of the split between the conscious and the unconscious mind. I say unconscious but, as I have already observed, strictly speaking there is nothing unconscious in the psyche. What exists are higher and lower voices which sing in a great polyphony. Except that this polyphony is sometimes closer to a cacophony in that the higher voices lead in one direction and the lower in another; the higher voices plan and desire one thing and the lower voices lag behind – my conscious mind may want health while my unconscious mind wants sickness, my conscious mind may want life and my unconscious mind may desire death, my conscious mind may want to forgive but my unconscious refuses to co-operate. And at the very core of my being is the deepest voice of all which is that of the Spirit. Quite often I cannot hear this voice or I ignore it or I cannot distinguish it from the other voices. And the result again is cacophony and discord.

Mystical healing of this inner division begins with the call of love at the core of my being, at the centre of my soul. This is the voice of the Spirit calling to union through an obscure sense of presence or a deep interior silence or a longing for solitude or a simple desire for God. Hearing this voice I begin the inner journey which is joyful because it is filled with love but painful because, like Abraham, I must pass from the familiar to the unfamiliar, from a state of consciousness which enjoys one set of beautiful things to a state of consciousness which values another. I do not know where I am going; the territory is unfamiliar; I am entering into areas of the psyche that are ordinarily dormant and unconscious; I am listening to the deeper voices; my inner eye which formerly was asleep is beginning to awaken. Consequently, profound changes take place; I begin to see things in a new way; I may seem like a different person both to myself and to others. 'At . . . times,' writes St John of the Cross, 'a man wonders if he is being charmed, and he goes about with wonderment over what he sees and hears. Everything seems so very strange even though he is the same as always. The reason is that he is being made a stranger to his usual knowledge and experience of things . . .' (*Dark Night*, 2:9,5). In all this process I am growing and growing; my consciousness is being expanded and deepened; I am becoming more myself; the most profound areas of my psyche are being actuated and brought to life; I am finding an inner unity resembling the original justice of the Garden of Eden.

Yet conflicts necessarily arise because, as Shakespeare adroitly remarks, the course of true love never did run smooth. I cling to what is familiar and dread the journey to what is unfamiliar like the man who wants both to follow the ox and enjoy the pleasures of remaining in the forest. Moreover, as new layers of the so-called unconscious are opened I come to see that not everything in my psyche is beautiful – ugly things are released, things which shock and trouble, things I would prefer not to see. How am I to cope with them?

In the holy places of many Asian countries one can see a set or series of pictures depicting the life of the Buddha. In one of these pictures Shakamuni, the enlightened one, sits splendidly in the lotus bathed in celestial light, his features radiating majestic calm and peace and composure, while all around him are yawning beasts and crawling snakes and seductive women. And the serene enlightened one pays absolutely no attention to these diabolical distractions. He does not fear the beasts; he is not seduced by the women. He tranquilly continues his inner journey to the depths of his being, to the great goal of mystery called nirvana.

And this is what we must do. Pay no attention to those beasts – they cannot harm you if you do not meddle with them. Let the lewd women smile alluringly – they cannot seduce you if you ignore them. Laugh at the snakes – they are illusory.

Yet great storms do arise and they can shake us to the roots of our being. One can be almost overwhelmed by gusts of anger or by nameless anxiety and fear, or by tumultuous sexuality, or by fierce rebellion against God and man. If a person has any neurotic tendencies (and most people have some) this is the time when they will appear, sometimes in a greatly intensified form. If parts of the psyche have been unfulfilled, this is the time when they will clamour for fulfilment. This may be the time when, precisely because of the inner turmoil, one loses friends or fails in one's work or does something so utterly stupid that one looks like an idiot in the eyes of all. And this may continue for a long time. It is not for me to decide when it will end – this is not in my power. But the *kairos* or time of deliverance will come.

The old authors spoke of the storm at sea when Jesus came to his disciples walking on the waters: 'They were frightened but he said to them, "It is I; do not be afraid" ' (John 6:20). This is a good illustration because the worst thing in this journey is fear or discouragement or despair. Do not be afraid. Do not be anxious. He will come walking on the waters and the storm will immediately cease and give place to a great calm.

Happy the person who in this situation finds a sympathetic friend who will encourage and console and help him to understand the situation and see what is happening. Happy the person who can come to accept this situation and to cry out with Paul: 'For the sake of Christ, then, I am content with weaknesses, insults, hardships, persecutions, and calamities; for when I am weak then I am strong' (2 Corinthians 12:10).

For the significant thing in this journey is the view of oneself – of one's own psyche with its weaknesses and its capacity for evil. Such an experience may be valuable in that it leads to compassion for others but it can also be very distressing. Those yawning beasts and slimy snakes and seductive women and grimacing devils – they are part of me. They are what Jung might call my shadow, the unacceptable parts of my personality with which I am now brought face to face. And what if secrets of the psyche are unlocked, secrets of my early childhood which I have refused to face – and now I get an untrammelled vision of self in fulfilment of those words of Jesus: 'Nothing is covered up that will not be revealed or hidden that will not be known' (Luke 12:2).

A moment ago I said that like the Buddha I must pay no attention to these monsters of the psyche. And now I repeat this. But let me add that in paying no attention I am coming to accept them and to accept myself as I am. And this self-acceptance is the first great key to integration of the personality. Once accepted many of these monsters will melt or disappear into the night – they were paper tigers anyhow. Yet this self-acceptance is only possible in view of the growing experiential conviction that I am loved by Another, profoundly loved. Yes, the first thing is not that I love but that I am loved, not that I give love but that I accept love.

Through this acceptance of self and of love I grow from childhood to adulthood. 'When I was a child, I spoke like a child, I thought like a child, I reasoned like a child; when I became a man, I gave up childish ways' (1 Corinthians 13:11). So in this healing process neuroses and hang-ups of all kinds melt away. One simply grows out of them, comes to look back on them from a higher vantage point – the problem may still be there but I see it in a new light and its crippling effects have vanished. I am moving towards that integration of the personality which Jung calls individuation.

III

I said that mysticism leads not only to union within oneself but also to union with all men. This is indeed so. But once again we are up against paradox: for union only comes through isolation and conflict.

In the early stages mystical experience often separates people from the crowd. They are out of step because they have heard a different drummer. Often they are for some time misfits in society, though they may have a few friends who understand them and share their aspirations. But the isolation is there, a painful consequence of the decision to follow the ox or to buy the field in which lies the treasure.

And yet, even while this separation is taking place, union with others is being enacted at another level. One reason for this is that all prayer, but especially contemplative prayer, leads to forgiveness and to the collapse of those unconscious barriers which cut us off from others. By barriers I mean things like suppressed anger, buried resentment, lack of forgiveness – all those neuroses which have existed in our unconscious since childhood or have even been inherited through the collective unconscious. Quite often these barriers are a neurotic relationship with one's parents.

Here let me digress for a moment to say that some modern psychologists have highlighted the supreme importance in human life of interior fidelity to the fourth commandment of the Decalogue – to love and honour one's parents. For relationship with parents (even when these parents are already dead) seems to be the key to success in other adult relationships. Nor can it be taken for granted that everyone honours his parents with an adult love. Quite often suppressed anger and resentment and fear and childish fixations linger on. And it is precisely here, in the deep, deep unconscious, that barriers fall down in the mystical journey. Love penetrates to the caverns of the unconscious, allowing the suppressed anger and fear and clinging to surface. Exposed to the light they melt away and a deep, adult ongoing love for one's parents becomes the basis for a universal love. Indeed, there can be an experience of enlightenment in which all barriers which separate me from others collapse and I discover that I am one with the human race, that no one is excluded from my compassion and love, that no rancour exists in my heart. This experience of union with the human race can be found, I believe, in the mysticism of all the great religions.

In Buddhism it is beautifully incarnated in the Bodhisattva Kannon whose statue stands magnificently throughout Asia. The name Kannon, literally Kan-ze-on, means 'beholder of the cries of the world' and this god or goddess (Kannon is originally a man but acquires the features of a woman and is often spoken of in feminine terms) with a gentle smile of compassion looks benevolently on all mankind. Kannon is one of the most beloved of Buddhist saints. But to return to my point.

Authentic mystical experience necessarily brings with it a great love for all mankind. It can lead to remarkably deep friendship and intimacy in those who share the same experience; it also leads to a great compassion for the poor, the sick, the oppressed, the down-trodden, the imprisoned, the underprivileged. Buddhist com-passion is an emptying of self in order to take to one's bosom the suffering people of the world; and Christian compassion is a dis-covery of Christ in the suffering people of the world. For he himself said: 'For I was hungry and you gave me food, I was thirsty and you gave me drink . . . as you did it to one of the least of my brethren you did it to me' (Matthew 25:35,40).

This union or solidarity with the poor and the oppressed is of the very essence of Christian mysticism. Even if the contemplative decides to spend his days in a solitary cave in the Himalayas or a tumbledown hut in the desert he is still united with the suffering world for which he intercedes and for which he offers his life. But not all mystics are on the mountain or in the desert. We find Christian mystics struggling for the liberation of the poor or picking up the dying in the streets of the big cities. This they do because they find Christ in the afflicted and become more and more closely united with him.

But again conflict! Love of the oppressed may bring one into con-flict with the rich and powerful and with the establishment. So it was with Jesus, so it will be with his followers.

It will be remembered that in the oxherding pictures the wise old man returns to the market-place to save all sentient beings. This is a picture of beautiful compassion. But I have sometimes felt that had the pictures been composed in the Christian West they would have ended with yet another picture which would hold the caption: *The Wise Old Man is Assassinated*. For the inner eye of this enlightened and compassionate sage would immediately see the terrible social injustice and the oppression of the poor. He would raise his voice in protest and even in holy anger, calling for liberation. And he would suffer the cruel fate of all the prophets from the just Abel to Martin Luther King.

And so union with Christ will mean union with the poor and the underprivileged and it will lead to conflict until such time as we reach the Omega point of convergence when Christ hands all to the Father and God is all in all. Until that time those who are united with Christ will be at odds with a large percentage of the human race.

'They are not of the world, even as I am not of the world' (John 17:14). And yet in a paradoxical way they will be united with the very people whom they criticize and against whom they fight. For they will love their adversaries and be united with the Christ in them, the Christ whose visage is often obscured and distorted but who lives in all men.

IV

I have spoken of inner union and the process of becoming another Christ. I have also spoken of union with the human race, particularly with the poor, through Christ. But all this is built on the deepest union of all: union with the Father through Christ.

To speak about this let me first return to the inner union about which I spoke at the beginning of this chapter, when I said that the deepest thing within us is the great mystery of mysteries which we call God – God who is the very ground and source of our being.

I said that the significant thing in this inner journey is a self-acceptance which is enacted at various levels. At one level there is myself with all my neuroses and complexes and capacity for evil and with my murky past – myself with my anxieties about health and reputation, myself with my irrational fear of rejection. When this self is accepted as loved (marvel of marvels!) at first through anguish and then with a sense of humour, there is another level of self: the existential level. Now I see myself as limited being, as being-towards-death, as potentially separated being. This is a whole new experience, a whole new level of existential anguish; and it can be terrible. Divorced from the totality, divorced from God I am *nothing*. All other human fears and anxieties are built on this realization of my own contingency – on the realization that I could be separated: 'My God, my God, why hast thou forsaken me?' (Matthew 27:46). This is the night of faith. I see myself as limited being, as separated being, all alone. Of course I believe and hope that I am united with God and with the totality; but this faith is dark and I feel totally and existentially alone. 'Oh my God, I cry by day, but thou dost not answer; and by night, but find no rest' (Psalm 22:2).

Now most people feel flashes of this existential anguish and loneliness at some time in their lives; but they escape from it to play tennis or watch television. But in the mystical life one is brought face to face with this fact of contingency. To see our own limitation and the possibility of separation from the totality which is God – this is to get a glimpse into hell. And it is truly terrible.

Mystics have sometimes spoken of the vision of hell; and we imagine big fires and little devils with pitchforks. This may be the artist's way of depicting it; but the reality is beyond words and images. The reality is a picture of contingent being isolated and separated from the whole. To see this possibility is an inevitable stage in the mystical life; it is an experience which is found in all the great religions. In Buddhism the most terrible thing imaginable is to build up one's ego and to be separated from the totality. This is the Buddhist hell. The doctrine of hell, like so much religious teaching, arises from the mystical experience of mankind.

But the vision of hell is not the end. For again he comes walking on the waters. 'It is I; do not be afraid' (John 6:20). And we realize not the separation from the totality but the identity with the totality. 'It is no longer I who live, but Christ who lives in me' (Galatians 2:20). This is Christ who dwells in the Father and who can say: 'I and the Father are one' (John 10:30). Through Christ and as another Christ I am one with the Father. Just as the vision of my separateness from the totality is hell, so the vision of my union with God is heaven.

We know little about God our Father. He is like night to the soul and he is surrounded by thick darkness. But one thing is clear; namely, that the higher stages of the mystical life are very ordinary. There is no ecstasy, no rapture, no flash of light, no bells, no incense. I am now my true self. It is sometimes said by Christian writers that the peak-point of mysticism is found in a vision of the Trinity. This is very true. But do not think of this vision of the Trinity as an extraordinary, earth-shaking vision of three in one. Not at all. It is a very simple and quiet realization that God is my Father and I, another Christ, am truly his son or his daughter and that the Holy Spirit dwells in me. This is the Christian self-realization. The Spirit who has transformed me, joins himself to my spirit and cries out: 'Abba, Father!'.

14. *Journey of Love*

I

Throughout this book I have stressed the fact that mysticism is a journey of love. It is the answer to a call of love; and every stage is enlightened and guided by a living flame, a blind stirring, a love which has no reservations or restrictions. This is the love which, Paul says, is superior to any charismatic gift and has no limitations whatsoever. It 'bears all things, believes all things, hopes all things, endures all things . . . love never ends' (1 Corinthians 13:7,8). And for Paul this is an incarnational love which is patient and kind, not jealous or boastful, not arrogant or rude.

This love burns at a very deep level of consciousness and is so different from what is ordinarily called love that perhaps we need a new word to describe it. The early Christians seem to have felt this need, and so they spoke of *agape*, a word which is little used in classical Greek. As for Buddhist mystics, they are reluctant to use the word love at all – since they feel that it scarcely fits the experience of nothingness which is fundamental to their lives. Yet I myself believe that *agape* exists in Buddhism and in Buddhist hearts. It is a question of getting clear what we mean by love.

II

The Christian mystics, then, speak constantly about love. But many (though not all) make use of the Song of Songs in a way which disturbs the exegetes and gives something of a Freudian shock to people like Dean Inge – who called the influence of the canticle 'deplorable'. And yet the man-woman motif keeps turning up in the Hebrew-Christian drama; and in our own day Bernard Lonergan (whom I have quoted abundantly) when he speaks of authentic religious experience returns to the theme of the bride and the bridegroom, speaking of 'other-worldly falling in love' and of the union of marriage. In this manner of speech he is part of a long tradition which goes back to the prophet Hosea in the eighth century BC and perhaps even further.

For Hosea, Yahweh is the bridegroom who loves his people

passionately and even foolishly in spite of their infidelity and harlotry. In his own private life the prophet has experienced all the pain and anger of rejection by the woman he loves and whom he has chosen as his bride. But he will still love her passionately and take her back to his bosom. And in the same way Yahweh tenderly loves his people and will call them back:

> I will heal their faithlessness
> I will love them freely
> (Hosea 14:4)

Some scripture scholars tell us that this Hosean description of the love of Yahweh was a scandal to those who first heard it; and they also tell us that while Yahweh 'loves' his people, the people do not 'love' Yahweh in precisely the same way. But in Deuteronomy (which was influenced by Hosea) Yahweh asks for a radical and unrestricted love when he speaks unequivocally to the people: 'Hear, O Israel: The Lord our God is one Lord; and you shall love the Lord your God with all your heart, and with all your soul, and with all your might' (Deuteronomy 6:4).

The bride–bridegroom theme is taken up by Jeremiah who writes about Israel's first love in the wilderness in contrast with her marital infidelity in the land of Canaan. And again in Isaiah: 'As the bridegroom rejoices over the bride, so shall your God rejoice over you' (Isaiah 62:5). In the New Testament, too, Jesus stands forth at Cana as the true bridegroom who changes the water into wine. And elsewhere he answers the Pharisees with the enigmatic words: 'Can the wedding guests mourn as long as the bridegroom is with them? The days will come, when the bridegroom is taken from them, and then they will fast' (Matthew 9:15). Jesus is the bridegroom and the people, the church, the community are his bride.

Underlying all this is the notion of a very powerful and unrestricted love of God for his people and the very total love which he asks in return. In the Bible this is framed in terms of God and the community; but from the early centuries of the Christian era we hear of the love affair between God and the individual devout soul. This way of speaking is found in Origen whose commentaries on the Song of Songs, translated by Jerome and Rufinus, were widely read in the West. It is also found in Augustine and Gregory and Cyprian; but the person most responsible for the wide diffusion of the bride–bridegroom theme is Bernard of Clairvaux whose *Sermons on the*

Canticle exerted incalculable influence on subsequent Christian spirituality. Consequently, we find this way of speaking in Bernard's younger contemporary Richard of St Victor and later in Jan Ruysbroeck, St Teresa of Avila, St John of the Cross and a great number of mystics.

As I have already said, this mystical use of the Song of Songs has been a source of embarrassment to many devout Christians. But let us remember that these love songs, like many literary masterpieces, can be read at different levels of consciousness; and let us also remember the wise observation of T. S. Eliot that there is more in the poetry than the poet himself realizes. For it is an undeniable fact that authentic mystics have read and reread the canticle with overflowing joy, have resonated with its vibrant sentences, have somehow identified with the passionate love described therein. They have felt deeply the wound of love and have exclaimed:

> You have ravished my heart, my sister, my bride,
> You have ravished my heart with a glance of your eyes
> (Song of Songs 4:9)

They have felt an immense longing which consumes their whole being and makes them cry out:

> Upon my bed by night
> I sought him whom my soul loves;
> I sought him, but found him not;
> I called him, but he gave no answer.
> I will rise now and go about the city,
> in the streets and in the squares;
> I will seek him whom my soul loves.
> (Song of Songs 3:1,2)

Such words have risen spontaneously to the lips of mystics after they have experienced a momentary enlightenment which, like a wound of love, has filled them paradoxically with ecstatic joy and with deep suffering. Where is he whom I love? They have been fascinated with a beauty which has touched them momentarily with such power that they have been forced to exclaim: 'Turn away your eyes from me for they disturb me' (Song of Songs 6:5).

Yes, the fact is that mystical experience, at one stage in its development, is a very passionate existential love which possesses the whole person, creating the most enormous thirst and longing for the infinite. Once touched by this love, people will travel the length and breadth of the earth, endure incredible suffering with joy, give up everything with a smile. This is the love which filled the heart of the psalmist when he cried: 'I stretch out my hands to thee, my soul thirsts for thee like a parched land' (Psalm 143). It is the love which inundated the heart of Paul when he exclaimed: 'My desire is to depart and be with Christ . . .' (Philippians 1:23).

Earlier in this book I said that all anguish is based on an existential anguish which is nothing other than the fear of contingent being separated from the totality. I said that this existential anguish in its pure form can be a vision of hell. And now let me add that just as there is an existential anguish at the root of all anguish, so there is an existential longing at the root of all longing. This is the love of contingent being for the totality, the love of the part for the whole, the love of the creature for the creator. Just as man is incomplete without the feminine – 'It is not good that man should be alone' (Genesis 2:18) – so contingent being is incomplete at the existential level without the totality. As man longs for woman and woman for man, so the human heart is restless until it rests in the totality.

Such is existential love. What is not often realized is that this love is an all-consuming and passionate fire which can envelop the personality and tear people asunder. It is particularly consuming and passionate in the heart of one who has experienced even to a small degree God's passionate love for him. If God has shown his face even for a moment, if he has unlocked the smallest of his secrets, if he has wounded my heart, then it is easy to make my own the words of the Song of Songs:

> Many waters cannot quench love,
>   neither can floods drown it.
> If a man offered for love
>   all the wealth of his house,
>   it would be utterly scorned
>   (Song of Songs 8:7)

I am speaking here in a Christian context; but I do not doubt that this same existential love exists in Buddhist mystics and in the mystics of all the great religions. Let us remember that in Buddhism the greatest evil is the desire for separate existence, and the longing for existential completeness is the greatest good. It is this existential longing that I speak about here.

Assuredly existential love need not be expressed in terms of the erotic; and many mystics do not appeal to the Song of Songs at all. But nevertheless it *is* frequently and persistently expressed in erotic man-woman language; and the question is asked: Why? What is the relationship between the erotic and the mystical?

Let me be frank and confess that I could never attempt to answer this question adequately and can do no more than add a few words of tentative explanation.

And first let me say that the existential love of which I speak is not purely spiritual. It has its roots in matter; it has its roots in the body; it does not reject physical or emotional or erotic love but simply goes beyond them, further and further beyond.

Now it is also true that in the passionate, romantic love with which the mystics resonate, this existential and universal dimension is already present. Hence the extravagant and hyperbolic expressions of lovers – protestations that their love is the greatest the world has known, that it will not die, that it is unrestricted. Such love differs from mystical love, however, in that it is not detached from its expressions; it is not detached from clinging and self-centredness; it is filled with projection; it is not open to the infinite. It may be, so to speak, mystical in embryo but it has to grow; and this can only happen through a process of detachment – through the emptiness, the nothingness, the void, the *mu*. All this nothingness does not kill love. By no means. It simply detaches it from its expressions and from its restrictions (for love is deeper and more mysterious than any of its expressions) so that it may be purified. In other words, the existential dimension which already exists in erotic love must grow, expand, develop until it is universal and unrestricted, open to man and God.

And so there is a process of growth from the erotic to the mystical. Jung traces this growth through symbols which are: Eve (biological love); Helen of Troy (romantic love); the Virgin Mary (devotional love); and Sapientia or Wisdom (mystical love). The idea of Jung is that, ideally speaking, human love should grow and develop through these stages – though he admits that in our day very few people reach the fourth and mystical stage.

Jung here speaks of masculine love for the feminine; but perhaps we could trace the growth in a way which would apply equally to men and to women. This would speak first of an *individual*, need love by which we love someone of the opposite sex in order to forget our loneliness. Next comes growth to *personal* love by which two people really share their being in a deep communion. Here there is more profound fulfilment, always joined to the danger that the two people may isolate themselves from society in a common solitude. Out of this they must break into a *cosmic* or *eternal* love in which the barriers of space and time are overcome and they are united with the cosmos, with Christ in one another and in all men, and with the Father.[1]

Such mystical love is incarnational in that man loves individual women and woman loves individual men. But extraordinary powers of loving have now been awakened so that they see the eternal incarnate in the temporal, the infinite incarnate in the finite: they see and love God in man. This means that in the face of the other they see Christ who is masculine as the *logos* and feminine as *sapientia*.

When love reaches this stage, however, it must go beyond the existential longing about which I spoke earlier. For it should be remembered that the existential longing of the contingent for the absolute is still based on need and is a form of spiritual passion. That is why Buddhists would be slow to accept it as the final stage in growth: it contains too much of the craving from which they wish to be liberated. Therefore we must go on and on – and there is yet another stage in which one is liberated from all craving, however spiritual, in order to love in complete liberty.

III

When it comes to describing the highest stage of love, the symbolism of the Fourth Gospel which speaks of father and son, and of friendship is extremely valuable.

Before speaking about the Fourth Gospel, however, let me recall that while the bride-bridegroom theme is found in the New Testament, it could scarcely be called central; and Jesus never uses it to describe his own mystical experience and his own union with God. No. Jesus always speaks of himself as Son; and his mystical experience is that of a son who loves his father and is loved by him.

[1] For a development of this theme see the excellent study of Juan Sanchez-Rivera Peiro: *Manifiesto de la Neuva Humanidad* (published by Ed. Paulinas, Madrid).

Furthermore, when Jesus teaches us to pray (and teaches us to pray mystically) he tells us to call God our Father. In other words, the central symbolism of the New Testament is not that of the bride and the bridegroom but of the father and the child.

Furthermore this is described by St John in terms of indwelling. In human life we know that mutual indwelling of friends is a fact of experience no less real than the love of the bride and the bridegroom. It sometimes happens that love so unites friends that despite miles of separation they are close to one another and dwell in one another. And when speaking of his relationship with his Father, Jesus keeps telling us that he dwells in the Father and the Father in him: 'Do you not believe that I am in the Father and the Father in me?' (John 14:10). Here is the mysticism of Jesus, a mysticism which extends to his friendships. For just as he dwells in the Father so his friends dwell in him. 'As the Father has loved me, so have I loved you; abide in my love' (John 15:9). Or again we have those striking, eschatological words: 'In that day you will know that I am in my Father, and you in me, and I in you' (John 14:20).

And so in the Fourth Gospel we get a remarkable picture of mystical union joined to the highest personalism. We dwell in Jesus; Jesus dwells in the Father; we all dwell in one another. We are completely one with God and others and the universe; and yet we become our truest selves, reaching the apex of human personalism and authenticity. And in this kind of indwelling there is a great absence of the clinging and craving and need which Buddhists regard as an imperfection in human loving.

Now I said earlier in this book and I repeat it now that the model of Christian mysticism is Jesus himself. As he is son by nature, we are sons or daughters by adoption. As he dwells in the Father, we dwell in the Father; as he dwells in us, we dwell in one another.

Concretely, the peak-point of mysticism in interpersonal relations is reached when we open the door of our hearts to a friend who is knocking in the name of the archetypal friend: 'Behold I stand at the door and knock; if anyone hears my voice and opens the door, I will come in to him and eat with him, and he with me' (Revelation 3:20). Yes, I hear the knocking on the door; but what freedom I have! I need not open; there is no compulsion; and if I refuse, even the best of friends must remain outside. But if I do open, there ensues an intimate indwelling and a loving banquet in which friends dine together without craving or clinging or dependence and without that exclusivity which is almost necessarily present in the bride-

bridegroom relationship. For such mystical friendship is not confined to one friend. It can embrace several people and leads to an indwelling in the Christ who identifies with the sick and the oppressed.

IV

Whatever symbolism is used, mystical love is never sterile but is intensely creative. We know from modern reflection on interpersonal relations that just as the physical union of man and woman creates the child, so the union of loving hearts can create great works of art and literature. This is an aspect of creativity which greatly claims the interest of modern people.

And mystical indwelling leads to creativity. Jesus says that his words and his actions are those of the Father who dwells in him: 'The words that I say to you I do not speak on my own authority; but the Father who dwells in me does his works' (John 14:10). And he speaks of the creativity of the disciples with the symbol of bearing fruit, fruit which will remain. The indwelling of Jesus in his disciples and of the disciples in Jesus is like the branch in the vine and the vine in the branch – this is a union which is always fruitful. In the same context Jesus speaks of the woman giving birth to her child. 'When a woman is in travail she has sorrow, because her hour has come; but when she is delivered of the child, she no longer remembers the anguish, for joy that a child is born into the world. So you have sorrow now . . .' (John 16:22).

The disciples to whom Jesus spoke would later bear their child. They would go out into that Mediterranean world with great joy and great love. Intensely creative people, they would build up something that would remain, a spiritual kingdom that will last to the end of time. This kingdom was born of their union with the Father through Jesus in the Spirit.

And so their work continues through the indwelling of God in man. Such union is *necessarily* creative: 'He who abides in me, and I in him, he it is that bears much fruit . . .' (John 15:5). The precise nature of this creativity in a given instance cannot be spelled out. For some will create the kingdom through love for the sick and dying, others through intellectual research, others through a passionate search for social justice, others through the silence of intercessory prayer and contemplation. There are varieties of gifts but the same Spirit of love inspires them all.

15. *Enlightenment and Conversion*

I have already indicated that the great fact on which Buddhism is built is the enlightenment of Shakamuni beneath the Bodhi tree at Bodh Gaya in the sixth century BC. This was an event which shook the world. And it is an event which has been repeated in the lives of Buddhists everywhere, even when they have belonged to different sects and to different cultures. Enlightenment is nothing other than the awakening of the third eye, the inner eye, the eye of the heart. This eye, represented in Indian culture by the round spot on the forehead, is single and sees the world of unity, as opposed to the two eyes of the flesh which see an illusory world of duality. When the inner eye is opened one enters the void or *sunyata* which is the realm of true wisdom, known as *prajna*. Here one is released from suffering and from the oppressive *karma* which has accumulated in this life and in past lives. In this way one is saved.

In some sects, such as Zen, enlightenment is achieved by personal effort (called *jiriki*); while in other sects, such as the Pure Land, one relies on the grace of another (*tariki*). But in either case enlightenment is an ongoing process. In some sects there are a series of sudden illuminations culminating in the supreme experience of Nirvana; in other sects illumination is a gradual process. Dogen, founder of the Soto sect of Zen, held that the very sitting is in itself an enlightenment. In this prolonged sitting in the lotus posture, one's consciousness is gradually changed and the inner eye comes to see.

What matters is the change of consciousness; and a good master can detect very rapidly the presence or absence of enlightenment in the consciousness of the one to whom he speaks. He may judge from the breathing or from the posture. Or he may ask questions and judge from the spontaneity (or lack of spontaneity) of the answer. I believe it is not too difficult to recognize the deeply enlightened consciousness: for the Buddhist who speaks from the depth of his own enlightenment has a humility, a compassion and an inner security which command respect and are quite different from the erudition of one who talks out of books.

Be that as it may, it is this enlightenment which attracts many people in the West; and sincere Christians ask to what extent they can participate in this Buddhist treasure which has been handed down from master to disciple through many centuries. This is a question which I have already discussed; and I need not repeat myself here.

II

The Gospel also speaks of enlightenment and Jesus refers to the eye of the heart when he says: 'The eye is the lamp of the body. So if your eye is sound, your whole body will be full of light; but if your eye is not sound, your whole body will be full of darkness. If the light in you is darkness, how great the darkness' (Matthew 6:22,23). Here we are told in no uncertain terms that what matters in life is illumination or enlightenment; and the same theme runs through the Fourth Gospel where the blind man comes to see that Jesus is the light of the world. We are that blind man and our life should be a sudden or gradual awakening. But the terrible thing is that as we can awaken so we can become blind. 'For judgement I came into the world, that those who do not see may see, and that those who see may become blind' (John 9:39). And so our life is a struggle against darkness. We possess the inner eye but we must awaken from sleep. 'Having eyes do you not see . . .?' (Mark 8:7).

But what do we see when our inner eye awakens? Here again the Fourth Gospel is clear:

We have seen his glory
(John 1:14)

The glory of the Risen Jesus cannot be seen with the eyes of the flesh but only with the eye of love. That is why Jesus rebuked Thomas who could not be satisfied until he saw Jesus with the eyes of the flesh; and Jesus says equivalently: 'Thomas, because you see with your physical eyes you are willing to worship me. But blessed are those who do not see with their physical eyes but see with their inner eye.' The awakening of this inner eye is a wonderful experience through which one comes to see 'the fullness of him who fills all in all' (Ephesians 1:23). One sees his glory in the cosmos; one sees his beauty on the faces and in the eyes of the friends one loves; one sees his suffering in the afflicted and oppressed.

Now the awakening to the reality of his glory is an authentic

Christian experience which has occurred frequently in Christian lives since Paul met Jesus on the road to Damascus. People have awakened to the stupendous fact that Jesus is the centre of their lives – that he truly is. Such an experience sometimes comes gradually, as one repeats the Jesus prayer and comes to realize that *Jesus is Lord*. Or it comes like a sudden shock at an unexpected moment when one experiences the glory of the Lord: 'If you confess with your lips that *Jesus is Lord* and believe in your hearts that God raised him from the dead, you will be saved' (Romans 10:9).

But the inner eye also sees the Father, for Jesus has said that he who sees him sees the Father also; and Paul assures us that every tongue will confess that 'Jesus is Lord *to the glory of God the Father*' (Philippians 2:11). In other words, when my inner eye is awakened and Jesus is the centre of my life I spontaneously look up to heaven and cry out: 'Abba, Father!'. This is the cry of the Spirit of Jesus within me. It is the Trinitarian experience about which I have spoken throughout this book. It is the Christian enlightenment.

III

I have spoken of enlightenment, but the Bible speaks also about conversion or *metanoia* or change of heart. This is a great revolution in human life which is described graphically by Ezekiel:

> A new heart I will give you and a new spirit I will put within you; and I will take out of your flesh the heart of stone and give you a heart of flesh. And I will put my spirit within you, and cause you to walk in my statutes and be careful to observe my ordinances.   (Ezekiel 36:26,27)

Here we have the radical change of mind and heart and body which is to find fulfilment in the Gospel cry: 'Change your hearts, for the kingdom of heaven is at hand' (Matthew 3:2). This is a theme which recurs throughout the symphony of Christian history. It is something very real in the Acts of the Apostles where people change their hearts and change their lives; it has been something very real wherever the Gospel has been preached. In Protestant theology it has always had a place of honour. Less so in Catholic theology until recently when Bernard Lonergan builds his *method* on this inner experience. As I have already said, Lonergan distinguishes religious, moral and intellectual conversion, thus pointing to a tremendous revolution in the personality. For by religious conversion one falls in love without restriction; by moral conversion one's values change; by intellectual conversion one sees into a world of being.

The process is well illustrated in the experience of Paul. He fell in love with Christ in an unrestricted way so that for Paul to live was Christ and to die was gain. His values changed in such a way that what he previously considered important is now like refuse compared with the great grace of knowing Christ Jesus his Lord. His outlook on life changed in such a way that he now sees a world no longer bounded by the law but without any horizons. His vision is now universal.

In the contemplative life as conceived by Buddhists and Christians alike, there are ordinarily periods of joy and consolation together with periods of darkness and boredom. There are also flashes of insight or illumination when one comes to understand some words of scripture or of revelation. But there may also be times of upheaval and inner revolution, times of momentous change when conversion is likely to occur. In other words, there are natural turning-points, crossroads or periods of crisis when the human psyche demands a conversion in its process of growth.

In this connection, Jung speaks of four crucial stages on the way to individuation or psychic fulfilment; and he calls them four births. The first is when the child leaves the womb of its mother and steps into life. The second is at puberty when the adolescent, liberating himself from parental authority and from psychic fusion with father and mother, enters adult life as an independently responsible person. The third is when the spiritualized person emerges from the conflicts of middle age and discovers his true self. The final stage is when man departs from the world and is born into the huge, unexplored land beyond death, the land from which he came.

Jung, however, believed that the majority of people do not pass successfully through these crises and are never fully born – principally because they fear the death which necessarily precedes birth. They shrink from the suffering and the pain; and so they are only born once and never reach integration.

Now I believe that the mystical life ordinarily develops through these Jungian stages of death and rebirth because in mysticism, as I have frequently stated, one does not transcend the human condition but becomes authentically human under the guidance of faith and love. Let me, then, consider here the third birth, that of middle age, which is particularly relevant for contemporary men and women.

In many of his writings but particularly in his autobiography *Memories, Dreams, Reflections*, Jung speaks about the death and re-birth which, ideally speaking, should take place through the crisis of middle age. Within us there are two personalities. Number one is the personality we show to the world, the person who in our youth and adolescence we think we are, the personality which becomes a doctor or a businessman or a teacher – our self-image derives from this personality. But much deeper than this slumbers another personality, number two, and here is the true self. Scarcely visible in early life, it is so smothered up by external things that only one who loves and understands us deeply can get a glimpse of it. We are not yet ourselves. But as life enters its middle period this deeper per-sonality awakens, begins to assert itself and to rise to the surface of consciousness. It is now that conflict begins.

Is number two friend or foe? This I do not know. I only know that number one is now captain of the ship and does not wish to lose control or to be dislodged. And yet certainly, if vaguely, I realize that number one must die if number two is to emerge into life. My old self must die if my new self is to be born. This can be an agonizing and fearful feeling; and it may precipitate a great crisis. This crisis is particularly acute if my vocation is at stake – if I fear that a wrong choice has been made and that fidelity to my deepest self may de-mand the adoption of a new path in life. Such a step may mean losing everything like Saint Paul who left a privileged position in his Jewish community to enter a world which he did not know.

This is indeed a great parting of the ways. Small wonder if many or most people, shrinking from the sacrifice involved, never allow their true personality to be born, never become their true selves. But, on the other hand, those who face up to the real issues find that the new personality is born with overwhelming joy. 'When a woman is in travail she has sorrow, because her hour has come; but when she is delivered of the child, she no longer remembers the anguish, for joy that a child is born into the world' (John 16:21).

At this point Jung half-humorously suggests that there should be schools for the middle-aged. And then he reflects that after all there are such schools: the great religions, if they do their work, are schools for the middle-aged. Here Jung has a real insight into the religious dimension of this great crisis. I believe that in this psychological turmoil grace is working gently, if painfully, in the unconscious, inviting our number two personality, our true selves, to emerge from the womb into fullness of life. Quite often this whole process of middle age crisis is nothing less than a mystical experience of death and resurrection to a new life which is filled with true joy.

I believe that the psychological process leading to deep conversion has something in common with that which frequently precedes great activity. Here a stillness or even a listlessness descends upon a person, as though power were being withdrawn from the conscious mind into the unconscious where it simmers for some time prior to a breakthrough into consciousness and the creation of great art or great scientific achievement or whatever. Conversion also is a creative process – for what is more creative than giving birth? – and it demands the marshalling of all the forces of the unconscious mind. But for the breakthrough to take place two conditions are ordinarily present.

The first is a period of solitude. This may be the solitude of a monastery or of a sick bed or of a prison cell. Or it may be hours and hours, days and days, of sitting in the silence of Zen. It is in this way that the upper layers of the mind are swept bare in preparation for the breakthrough of grace from the unconscious. In such a situation there is no escape from one's self, no escape from one's number two personality which is rising up to vanquish us and give us joy.

The second condition, as we have already seen, is some kind of shock. Remember that Paul was blinded and neither ate nor drank for three days. In other cases the shock may come from acute rejection which causes great pain. Think of the prophet Nathan pointing the finger at David: 'You are the man' (2 Samuel 12:7). And David was shaken to the core. 'And David said to Nathan: "I have sinned against the Lord" '(2 Samuel 12:13). Shocked into self-realization! Or again when Peter protested against the suffering of his master, and Jesus turned on him: 'Get behind me, Satan! For you are not on the side of God but of men' (Mark 8:33). For Peter it must have been a profound shock to be treated in this way by the Master he loved. But it had to be. His way of thinking was wrong; he did not understand the Cross; and only the deep pain of apparent rejection by Jesus could awaken him to the way of thinking that is of God.

And so a great rejection, especially rejection by those we love, can precipitate death and herald the joy of resurrection. Only in this context can I understand the words of Jesus: 'Blessed are you when men revile you and persecute you and utter all kinds of evil against you falsely on my account. Rejoice and be glad, for your reward is great in heaven . . .' (Matthew 5:11,12). Taken as a command to rejoice in rejection these words might sound inhuman; but seen in the light of *metanoia*, seen in the light of death and resurrection, they are the quintessence of wisdom and enlightenment. Rejoice and be glad because the pain of rejection is the herald of unutterable joy.

The art, the cruel yet compassionate art, of shocking a person into enlightenment is part of authentic spiritual direction in all religions and is well known to the skilled master in the Orient. Not that he shocks for the sake of shocking – that would be disaster – but he sternly confronts the disciple with the vision, the true vision, of his self in its inadequacy and weakness. 'You are the man!' 'You are not on the side of God but of men!' And the painful view of the truth, the painful view of death and of hell, tears away the veil of illusion and leads to the joyful vision of a total truth which heralds resurrection.

To shock into enlightenment is, as I have said, a great art. Only the person of powerful insight, rigorous detachment and profound compassion can kill and change death to life.

IV

I have said that fidelity to one's deepest self, to one's number two personality, may demand the choice of a new path. This is often the most distressing aspect of this crisis and conversion. For who wants to be uprooted in his middle years? Yet such was the case with St Paul. Such was the case with John Henry Newman: 'Lead, kindly light!' And this is an anguishing choice which confronts not a few religious people in our troubled times. When my true personality rises to the surface, will it demand that I change my state in life?

In the *Spiritual Exercises* (where St Ignatius intends primarily to lead the exercitant to conversion and choice of a state in life) this problem is faced squarely. And Ignatius insists from the beginning that there are certain immutable decisions or irrevocable choices in human life which cannot even be reconsidered. Most people would agree with this. A decision which involves the happiness of other people cannot lightly be revoked – unless I do so out of fidelity to truth which must always be obeyed. But still, in our complex age it is by no means easy to say which decisions are irrevocable and which are not.

. Here I cannot enter into the complex ethical controversies which have arisen on this point. What I want to say is that there is a solution which arises from the depth not of an ethical, but of a religious, conversion. That is to say, a solution that is connected with my falling in love without restriction and is nothing less than a religious enlightenment. Let me explain what I mean.

The solution I speak of depends upon prayer, upon prolonged prayer like that of Jesus in the wilderness. And I believe that if one devotes oneself to this prolonged prayer in silent non-attachment, the answer will come not from ethical reasoning but from the Spirit who dwells in the depth of the so-called unconscious. The enlightenment which thus arises will not be an ethical one: it will not tell us that this path is morally correct and the other wrong. Rather will it be a vision of the truth which makes us free. For a Buddhist it may be a moment of profound enlightenment after which he sees with great clarity what he should do. For a Christian it may be a great upsurge of love which makes him cry out: 'Jesus is Lord'. And then, as a second step, love will tell him what to do. Or it may be something much less dramatic. Just a quiet realization repeated again over weeks and months, always accompanied by joy and consolation, giving birth to a conviction that the Spirit has spoken.

As can be seen, I am here distinguishing between the ethical and the religious conversion. I am trying to say that the religious happening will often come first and that the ethical decision will flow from it. But this is always the work of grace.

V

I have spoken about conversion but one may ask about its contrary. What about breakdown? What about counter-conversion?

One aspect of breakdown, I believe, is simply the refusal to grow, the refusal to allow the true personality to emerge, the refusal to be born. This means that I get stuck at a lower level of psychic development and never allow myself to be fully born. I do not use my talents: much of my potential remains untapped. To some extent this is the fate of all of us; we shrink from the suffering entailed in conversion; we run away from the hound of heaven. And so we are never fully born; we never realize our full potential.

This is sad. But there can be something more terrible; namely, a breakthrough to evil, a conversion in reverse. For just as grace works in the unconscious gradually leading to enlightenment and a change of heart for good, so in the same way evil can gradually build up to a breakthrough into consciousness and a change of heart for evil. And this, too, could be accompanied by great joy – a conversion to evil, an enlightenment from Satan.

St Ignatius indicates this in the *Spiritual Exercises* when he says that those who go from evil to evil are drawn on by Satan *with consolation*. This is because diabolical influence is, so to speak, in harmony with their inner dispositions and so it comes as a sweet messenger of joy: 'When the disposition is similar to that of the (evil) spirits, they enter silently, as one coming into his own house when the doors are open' (Ignatius (1), p. 149). When the dedication of such people to evil is total, the counter-conversion is complete. Now they experience security and peace in the accomplishment of evil. This is a terrible consideration. One is reminded of the First Epistle of John which, speaking about prayer for sinners, goes on to say that some sin is so deadly that we need not bother praying for it: 'There is sin which is mortal; I do not say that one is to pray for that' (1 John 5:16). At this stage of dedication to evil only great grace can effect conversion. But grace is always present.

Finally let me say a word about group conversion. This surely seems to be the great need of our day, a time of upheaval and revolution; and the Second Vatican Council made a call for communal conversion.

Such conversion took place when the Spirit descended upon the apostles at Pentecost. But I believe that such Pentecosts are rare. More often the salvation of the group is achieved through the conversion of the few. 'For the sake of ten I will not destroy it' (Genesis 19:32). There are people who, following Jesus in Gethsemane, take upon themselves the suffering of the world. We need such people today. What the future holds we do not know.

PART IV

MYSTICAL ACTION

16. *Towards Action*

I have already indicated that mystical action flows from *wu-wei* or non-action. It is not based on reasoning and thinking and conscious effort but rather on letting things happen, letting the Tao act, letting God work in me and in the world. In a Christian context, mystical action reaches its climax when I surrender to the Spirit so totally that I can make my own the words of Paul: 'It is no longer I who live but Christ who lives in me' (Galatians 2:20). When these words live in me the Spirit of Jesus governs my life, my action is no longer my own, and what appears to be conscious effort is the activity of a deeper power which dwells within. All I have to do is to accept. Was not one of the world's greatest decisions made by one who said: 'Behold, I am the handmaid of the Lord; let it be done to me according to your will' (Luke 1:38)? Here conscious effort fell into the stream of non-action.

But submission to the Spirit is an art which is only learned through years of trial and error, success and failure. Only gradually does one come to possess a delicate sensitivity to the inner motions of grace so as to be moved by the Spirit in one's life. And the art or gift by which we come to recognize the inner voice of the Spirit is called discernment.

Discernment is of the essence of mysticism in action. The medievals were greatly interested in it, and they kept asking a number of simple but intriguing questions: How am I to know when to eat and when to fast, when to sleep and when to watch, when to go into solitude and when to go into action. How am I to discern the voice of the Spirit so as to follow his gentle guidance? And of course they could ask even more weighty questions like those I discussed in the last chapter – questions about vocation and state of life.

Such weighty and even agonizing questions are confronting sincere people in our day – people who work in the world of science or of business or of politics. Such people may be called on to make decisions which will affect the lives of millions of men and women. Often these decisions cannot be made through unquestioning obedience to ethical laws but only through a process of discernment and listening to the Spirit. But how am I to discern the voice of the Spirit in my life?

II

A great master of discernment was Ignatius of Loyola. His experiments (if I may call them that) began when he was a young soldier, wounded in the leg at the siege of Pamplona and compelled to lie on a sick bed in a lonely Spanish castle. Out of sheer boredom and because there was nothing else available, he began to read the lives of the saints and then (and here is the interesting thing) *he began to listen to himself*. He began to listen to his own feelings which were sometimes joyful and sometimes sad. He himself describes in the third person what happened:

> When he was thinking of the things of the world *he was filled with delight*, but when afterwards he dismissed them from weariness *he was dry and dissatisfied*. And when he thought of going barefoot to Jerusalem and of eating nothing but herbs and performing the other rigours he saw that the saints had performed, he was consoled, not only when he entertained these thoughts, but even after dismissing them he remained cheerful and satisfied. But he paid no attention to this, nor did he stop to weigh the difference until *one day his eyes were opened a little* and he began to wonder at the difference and to reflect on it, learning from experience that *one kind of thought left him sad and the other cheerful*. Thus, step by step, he came to recognize the difference between the two spirits that moved him, the one being from the evil spirit, the other from God.   (Ignatius (2), p. 10)

Here Ignatius listens to himself, listens to his own feelings of consolation and desolation, and on the basis of this he eventually makes the greatest decision of his life; namely, to give up 'the things of the world' and to travel barefoot to Jerusalem. This, in turn, is a symbol of a deeper decision to dedicate himself totally to Christ.

Now the practice of listening to one's own feelings is advocated by a number of modern psychologists. Jung, particularly in his later years, spoke about listening to his *anima* or feminine principle and, needless to say, he was constantly listening to what the unconscious was saying through dreams. More recently Carl Rogers advocates attention to, and acceptance of, one's feelings. 'I find myself more effective,' he writes, 'when I listen acceptantly to myself, and can be myself. I feel that over the years I have learned to become more adequate in listening to myself; so that I know, somewhat more adequately than I used to, what I am feeling at any given moment – to be able to realize that I *am* angry, or that I *do* feel rejection towards this person; or that I feel very full of warmth and affection for this individual; or that I am bored and uninterested in what is going on; or that I am eager to understand this individual or that I am anxious and fearful in my relationship to this person. All of these diverse attitudes are feelings which I think I can listen to in myself. One way of putting this is that I feel I have become more adequate in letting myself be what I am.'[1]

For Carl Rogers, listening to one's feelings is a way to fullness of life and to the actuation of one's potentialities. But it is more than this. The great psychologist maintains that the process of listening to one's self leads to right action or (to use his terminology) to the good life. It is precisely in obeying one's deepest self, one's total self, that one's actions become truly human. This is because man's basic nature is positive and trustworthy. In this regard I would like once more to quote some of his words:

> One of the most revolutionary concepts to grow out of our clinical experience is the growing recognition that the innermost core of man's nature, the deepest layer of his personality, the base of his 'animal nature' is positive in nature – is basically socialized, forward moving, rational and realistic . . . This point of view is so foreign to our present culture that I do not expect it to be accepted . . . Religion, especially Protestant Christian tradition, has permeated our culture with the concept that man is basically sinful, and only by something approaching a miracle can his sinful nature be negated. (Rogers, p. 91)

Quite frankly, the above astonished me. To me what Carl Rogers

---

[1] (Rogers, p. 17.) In the same book, Rogers writes of the good life: 'The individual is becoming more able to listen to himself, to experience what is going on within himself. He is more open to his feelings of fear and discouragement and pain. He is also more open to his feelings of courage, and tenderness, and awe. He is free to live his feelings subjectively, as they exist in him, and also free to be aware of these feelings. He is more able fully to live the experiences of his organism rather than shutting them out of awareness' (p. 188).

has discovered is not revolutionary at all. I had always taken it for granted that man's basic nature is good since he was created in the image of God. Moreover I was educated in a Thomist philosophy which taught something similar to what Rogers is saying; namely, that the norm of morality is human nature and that by obeying the fundamental dictates of human nature one's activity is right. Original sin, of course, is there. But it is a wound which weakens, without corrupting, human nature. I believe that all the great religions hold ultimately that man's basic nature is good since at the core of his being is Brahman or Atman or the Buddha nature or the Holy Spirit.

Coming, however, to religious discernment, one might reasonably ask how it differs from the listening to one's feelings advocated by psychologists like Carl Rogers.

And to this I would answer that in religion new elements enter in.

The first new element is faith. Religious faith had taught Ignatius and those like him that the Spirit who dwells in the depth of our being guides and directs and comforts and teaches, as is written in the Fourth Gospel. It further taught him the reality of sin. While it is true that human nature is fundamentally good, we cannot take it for granted that the lives of all men and women are orientated towards good; there is the possibility of choosing sin and evil. Again, faith taught Ignatius that there are forces of evil outside man and distinct from man. These he calls evil spirits.

Consequently, while Ignatius is aware of his feelings and interior movements in a way that reminds one of Jung and Rogers, he differs from them in his great preoccupation with *the origin* of these feelings and with *their goal*. And so he asks further questions: Are these inner movements from the spirit of love who dwells within and guides me towards love? Or are they from the evil spirit? Or are they from my little ego? Will the following of this inner stirring lead me to a life of unrestricted love or will it isolate me in a loveless solitude? Are these feelings leading to *metanoia* or to breakdown?

To answer these questions, says Ignatius, I must first investigate my basic dispositions. If my thrust is towards evil (which God forbid!) then these so-called positive feelings of joy and consolation may be confirming me in my evil path. If, on the other hand, I am basically orientated towards good (and I have no doubt that all of my readers are) then feelings of joy and consolation are a sign of the action of the Spirit. In short, my basic disposition is of crucial importance.

But even when my basic dispositions are good, I still must scrutinize my thoughts, asking myself in what direction they are leading me, since self-deception is always possible. 'We must carefully observe the whole course of our thoughts. If the beginning and middle and end of the course of thoughts are wholly good and directed to what is entirely right, it is a sign that they are from the good angel. But the course of thoughts suggested to us may terminate in something evil, or distracting, or less good than the soul had formerly proposed to do. Again, it may end in what weakens the soul, or disquiets it; or by destroying the peace, tranquillity, and quiet which it had before, it may cause disturbance to the soul. These things are a clear sign that the thoughts are proceeding from the evil spirit, the enemy of our progress and eternal salvation' (Ignatius (1), p. 148).

Yet another element which psychology does not ordinarily take into account is the presence of mystical experience. As I have already indicated, this is an experiential and undeniable psychic fact which has been described as a living flame of love, a blind stirring of love, an obscure sense of presence, a murmuring stream, a small fire, the voice of the Spirit and so on. And in the mystical life listening to one's feelings means above all hearkening to this deepest of all feelings. The important thing is to be faithful to this and to act in harmony with its promptings. When I do so, I feel joy and peace and security, even in the midst of conflict and suffering. When I act against it I immediately feel upset and inner turmoil.

The medievals urge us to be constantly attentive to this inner flame. 'Hold yourself at the sovereign point of the spirit!' is the good advice of the author of *The Cloud*. That is to say, remain at the level of awareness where the flame of love is living. Do not be carried away by superficial feelings of any kind – be they feelings of joy or sadness, of elation or depression. If you remain poised at this deep point of recollection and at the ground of your being, Satan will not be able to disturb you (for he cannot enter these innermost mansions) and you will be open to the directives of the Spirit. Indeed, a time will come, says St John of the Cross, when the inner flame will tell you what to do in your daily life. Speaking of advanced contemplatives the Spanish mystic writes: 'For God's Spirit makes them know what must be known and ignore what must be ignored, remember

what ought to be remembered . . . and forget what ought to be forgotten, and make them love what they ought to love, and keeps them
from loving what is not God (*Ascent*, 3:2,9). And he adds an example:
'At a particular time a person will have to attend to a necessary
business matter. He will not remember through any form, but
without knowing how, the time and suitable way of attending to it
will be impressed on his soul without fail' (*Ascent*, 3:2,11).

And yet such a stage of mystical union is not common. Ordinarily we must search for the voice of the Spirit, sometimes with
anguish. Quite often we are in illusion or bogged down by in-
decision. At other times we are completely in the dark. Consequently,
to aid us in the process of discernment the Christian tradition
worked out a whole science which is still alive today.

III

The science of discernment has its roots in the New Testament. The
early Christians were aware of the movements and stirrings which
arise in the human heart and in the human community; and they
asked about the spirits from which these movements originated.
'Beloved,' writes St John, 'do not believe every spirit, but test the
spirits to see whether they are of God; for many false prophets have
gone into the world' (1 John 4:1). In other words, do not follow your
feelings and whims indiscriminately, however pious and holy they
may appear – you might easily deceive yourself. So test the spirits.
And John goes on to give a clear-cut norm:

> By this you know the Spirit of God: every spirit which con-
> fesses that Jesus Christ has come in the flesh is of God, and every
> spirit which does not confess Jesus is not of God. (1 John 4:2,3)

From this it is clear that 'Jesus' is the first norm: Jesus who has
come in the flesh. The same idea is found in Paul. 'Therefore I want
you to understand that no one speaking by the Spirit of God ever
says "Jesus be cursed" and no one can say "Jesus is Lord" except by
the Holy Spirit' (1 Corinthians 12:3).

'Jesus is Lord' was, as we have seen, one expression of faith and of
metanoia. And this Jesus was not only the risen Jesus who is lord of
the cosmos but also the Jesus who has come in the flesh and is
present in his brethren, the Jesus who taught that blessed are the
poor and the meek and the merciful and the peace-lovers and the

persecuted. Consequently, we can say that the New Testament norm is very practical. It means that thoughts and deep feelings of compassion for the poor, the sick, the underprivileged and the rejected; joyful desires of poverty and even of persecution with Jesus persecuted – in short whatever is in conformity with the Gospel of Jesus Christ – is from the spirit of God; whereas thoughts and feelings which lead to rejection of Jesus, to hatred of his brethren, to dissension and violence, to lust for money and power – these are not from the Spirit of God. Elsewhere in the New Testament Paul is to spell this out when he speaks of the works of the flesh and the works of the Spirit: 'Now the works of the flesh are plain: immorality, impurity, licentiousness, idolatry, sorcery, enmity, strife, jealousy, anger, selfishness, dissension, party-spirit, envy, drunkenness, carousing and the like ... But the fruit of the Spirit is love, joy, peace, patience, kindness, goodness, faithfulness, gentleness, self-control' (Galatians 5:19–23).

As can at once be seen the norm of morality in the New Testament is not fidelity to the law but fidelity to the Spirit – that is fidelity to the law of love which includes every other law since 'love is the fulfilling of the law' (Romans 13:10).

The science of discernment was developed by the Church fathers; and later, in the Middle Ages, we find the author of *The Cloud* composing a charming treatise on discernment of stirrings. And to this same tradition belongs Ignatius.

The young soldier about whom I have spoken, later elaborated a whole mysticism of action based on a sensitivity to the presence of God and the working of the Spirit. Two further points in his mysticism are worth noting.

The first is his stress on what he calls *indifference*. This simply means holding oneself poised at the sovereign point of the spirit, ready to follow the voice of the beloved in whatever direction it may call. But to maintain such a position one must be liberated from inordinate affections and one must possess an inner liberty which is not unlike the non-attachment demanded by Buddhist mysticism.

The second is that Ignatius always recommended a rational check. That is to say, he asks us to bring our conclusions before the bar of reason, insisting that any feelings which run contrary to reason cannot be from God.

The disciples of Ignatius further elaborated his doctrine; and we find the Jesuit, Louis Lallement, who is representative of a school of Jesuit mysticism in seventeenth-century France, advocating this same inner awareness as a way of life.

> Let us watch with care the different movements of our soul. By such attention we shall gradually perceive what is of God and what is not. That which proceeds from God in a soul subjected to grace is generally peaceable and calm. That which comes from the devil is violent, and brings with it trouble and anxiety.
>
> (McDougall, p. 109)

And so we have a way of life in which one is always open to the inner vibrations and in touch with one's deepest feelings. It presupposes what modern people call 'emotional honesty'. That is to say, I recognize the movements that are within me and even give them a name, admitting that I am angry or lustful or fearful, or that I am joyful or optimistic or courageous.

Ignatius spoke frequently of *examination of conscience* and he recommended that people examine their conscience again and again and again during the day. This, alas, was taken in an ethical sense, as though we ought constantly to accuse ourselves of sins and defects of all kinds. But more recently a whole new interpretation of this process has been made, an interpretation which is surely more faithful to Ignatius. For now we hear not of *examination of conscience* but of *examination of consciousness*. Obviously this is healthier. And it leads to a constant awareness of the action of the Spirit in one's life.

I have said that discernment is nothing less than a way of life and the very basis of mysticism in action. It is something that goes on all the time. One is constantly open to the breath of the Spirit, to the action of God in one's life and in the world; one is always poised in readiness to hear the voice of the beloved and to follow where it leads. This is one's daily bread and one's food: 'My food is to do the will of him who sent me, and to accomplish his work' (John 4:34). But there will, of course, be special times – times when great decisions arise. And then, as Jesus prayed for forty days in the wilderness before beginning his ministry, as he prayed all night before choosing his disciples, as he prayed in Gethsemane before his passion, it will be necessary to pray, to reflect, to consult with others, to search out the divine will.

IV

From what has been said it will be clear that for discernment we need an objective view of ourselves and our feelings. As long as we are entangled in our own anger or vanity or lust or fear or craving we cannot be poised and ready to follow the call of the Spirit of love. How, then, can we attain to this objectivity and inner freedom?

The principal way is by prayer and reflection on the meaning of life, thus deepening our inner experience and entering into a new level of awareness where craving and attachment no longer tyrannize our lives. But it is also useful to write a journal or to sketch or to paint or to engage in any creative art. For this has the effect of objectifying our thoughts and feelings and of liberating us from their domination. All this is good. But when all is said and done, I believe there is no substitute for opening one's soul to another – to one who accepts, who loves, who listens, who does not judge, who reflects back to me what is in my mind and heart, who helps me to recognize the voice of the Spirit in my life.

This is spiritual guidance. It differs from counselling in that it is a *religious experience* enacted between two people. That is to say, it is the experience of two people who are in love without reservation or restriction and who meet at the level of psychic life where the Spirit of God dwells. Such a religious experience exists in an authentic relationship between master and disciple. It exists in its painful, yet loving, form when the master shocks his disciple into self-realization. But ordinarily he does not do this. He accepts; he listens; he loves; he shares. Sometimes he says nothing; and then there is a bond of silence which unites more deeply than words and communicates immense wisdom. The master gives and receives the Holy Spirit – because this is a two-way path, a mutual giving and receiving.

Such a relationship can become extremely deep and can develop into a mystical friendship. For the time may come when the master finds that he is no longer a master. He must make his own the words of one who said: 'No longer do I call you servants . . . but I have called you friends, for all that I have heard from my Father I have made known to you' (John 15:15). In this way, the relationship becomes one of equality, of mutual indwelling and of common indwelling in God.

The art of discernment is still developing; and I believe it will be of cardinal importance in the decades which lie ahead. This is because, as I have said, complex and difficult decisions are arising in the lives of good people and a legalistic ethic is unable to cope with them. In the evolution of discernment I see two important factors.

The first is dialogue between spirituality and modern psychology. As we all know, an outstanding characteristic of modern culture is its discovery of, and appreciation for, human feeling. By feeling I do not just mean emotion but the deeper and more subtle inner movements of the psyche, which have been analysed and clarified as never before. Moreover, the movement which stems from Carl Rogers and others to love oneself, to accept one's feelings, to trust one's feeling, to love one's body – all this will teach many and valuable lessons to spirituality and to religions.

The second factor is Christian dialogue with Buddhism. For the art of listening to one's body and one's feelings and even to one's thoughts and one's innermost spiritual activities is highly developed in Buddhist meditation and is called *mindfulness*. About this I will speak later in this book. Here only let me say that one becomes aware of one's breathing, of one's body, of one's feelings, of one's thoughts. In this total awareness, one experiences an inner liberation in such a way that one is not dominated or controlled by inner craving of any kind. Yet all the time one accepts these feelings and listens to them with great objectivity. Moreover, in this kind of meditation one learns to listen not only to the feelings but also to the body. And there is enormous wisdom in the body. It can tell us when to eat and when to fast, when to sleep and when to watch. But we must learn how to listen!

By watching the body and the breathing and the posture a skilled Oriental master can learn a lot, almost everything, about the spiritual attainment of his disciple. That is why he often needs no words. And we, too, can learn to listen to the Spirit through our own bodies and that of others. Here is an important field for discernment in the years which lie ahead.

17. *Intercession*

I

If the modern world is interested in meditation it is also greatly fascinated by the prayer of petition. This is partly because contemporary man, efficient, practical and materialistic, has suddenly awakened to the fact that intercessory prayer gets results. Things happen. The sick are healed, the sun begins to shine, projects that looked hopeless start to prosper. Surely this is worth investigating! And so we find parapsychologists conducting experiments on plants and fields of wheat. People pray for growth in some fields while other fields are left unprayed for – and the results are carefully tabulated. On the basis of this and other evidence, theories have been elaborated about spiritual vibrations, subtle energy and the rest. Is there, after all, in the universe a form of energy as yet unknown to science?

How far these speculations are valid I do not know. It is not impossible that subtle, spiritual vibrations are at work and that science will some day tap an energy which is now unknown to us. But even if it does, I believe that even deeper than this and at the root of all is the great mysterious power of God which no scientific instrument will ever touch. This is the power which we call grace; and it is associated with faith and love.

But quite apart from all this, the great religions attach the utmost importance to the prayer of intercession. In one sect of Buddhism which has recently become extremely popular in Japan, believers chant again and again the mantra: 'Honour to the lotus sutra'; and it is claimed that the vibrations thus aroused tap the life-force which governs the activity of the whole universe.[1] This means that by reciting these words with faith and perseverance one can achieve remarkable results. Devout believers kneel before their sacred scroll chanting the mantra thousands and thousands of times for the success of their projects, for the prosperity of their business, for the triumph of their political party, and for world peace.

This kind of belief is closely associated with the Oriental notion of *karma*. Just as the pebble thrown into the pond causes ripples

[1] The formula *Namu-Myoho-renge-kyo* is used by many branches of the Nichiren sect.

that extend to the bank, so every thought and action has its ripples throughout the whole universe. In consequence, no prayer or aspiration is wasted but is always resounding through aeons of existences. But likewise (and this is more sobering) no evil deed or thought is without its sad consequences. Believers in *karma* are confirmed in their conviction by the modern scientific notion of a close-knit universe in which the tiniest movement of one particle exercises influence on the whole.

In this form of Buddhism words are used. But words are not necessary. The silent sitting in meditation itself communicates wisdom and goodness to all men, and we find a Buddhist saying: 'The sun radiates its splendour on all alike: in like manner the *tathagata* radiates the truth of noble wisdom without recourse to words on all alike.' Surely this is a beautiful picture of the enlightened one communicating wisdom and goodness to the whole world.

Yet another altruistic prayer, practised in the East and now adopted by some Christians, centres around the breathing. One sits cross-legged and breathes goodwill to the whole universe. With the exhalation of each breath I send out vibrations of love and compassion to all men and women and to all living creatures. This is beautiful. But it should be noted that it presupposes a certain degree of interior purification. We are warned to take care lest we breathe out our anger and frustration and hatred and envy. The moral is: get rid of all that first and then breathe out love and compassion.

Granted, however, that some degree of inner purification is effected, we can intercede for friends by breathing the Spirit to them – imagining that they are present and that we are imposing hands on them, communicating the Spirit as did Jesus when he breathed on his disciples saying: 'Receive the Holy Spirit. If you forgive the sins of any, they are forgiven . . .' (John 20:23). I know Christians who pray in this way, communicating the Spirit to their friends, always returning to Christ who is the source from whom the Spirit flows. Indeed, through breathing with faith the Spirit can be communicated to the minds and hearts and bodies of others.

II

In the Hebrew-Christian tradition the prayer of intercession has pride of place. Never think that one, so to speak, grows beyond the prayer of petition to enter into the cloud of mystical prayer – as though intercession were for beginners and mysticism for proficients. Not at all. For at the head of the Hebrew tradition stands Moses the mediator, praying for his people with outstretched arms. The great prophet is the type and forerunner of Jesus, the mediator between God and man. As Moses prayed for Aaron, so Jesus prays for Peter: 'Simon, Simon . . . I have prayed for you that your faith may not fail' (Luke 22:32). Remarkable words! Where and when did Jesus pray for Peter? Perhaps Peter's name arose in his mind during those long nights when, alone on the mountain, he prayed to his Father for the world. Again, in that long, priestly prayer in the seventeenth chapter of the Fourth Gospel, Jesus intercedes for his disciples and for us who are their disciples – before praying for himself in Gethsemane and offering his life to the Father on the Cross: 'Father, into thy hands I commit my spirit' (Luke 23:46).

And we are told to ask and to keep asking – for ourselves and for others. 'Ask, and it will be given you; seek, and you will find; knock, and it will be opened to you' (Matthew 7:7). But it is important that the asking spring not from our little ego but from the Spirit who dwells within us. That is why Jesus tells us to ask *in his name*. Not in our name but in his name. 'Hitherto you have asked nothing in my name; ask and you will receive, that your joy may be full' (John 16:24). It sometimes takes discernment to find out in whose name we ask. It may be that we are asking in our own name; and then the prayer lacks conviction and quickly peters out. But at other times the prayer arises constantly and perseveringly with the unshakeable conviction that it will be heard – and this is the prayer which comes from the indwelling Spirit. St Teresa of Avila speaks of occasions in which the inspiration to pray for another rose spontaneously and unexpectedly in her heart. It was as though she was not deciding who she would intercede for: that decision was made by another. This is prayer in his name. This is prayer with faith.

And so throughout the centuries the Christian community has raised its voice to God our Father asking for daily bread, for forgiveness of sin, and to be delivered from evil. And the prayer is always heard. Just as Eastern religions speak of a life-force which runs through all things and unites all beings in the universe, so Christians speak of a living breath of love, a Spirit who dwells in the whole world and in the hearts of men and women everywhere. It is because we are all united in the Spirit that prayer in Tokyo has repercussions in New York, and intercession in Delhi affects Berlin. We are one in the spirit, always affecting one another.

If I were asked to speak of a mystic who uses intercessory prayer, I would immediately quote Paul. The opening verses of his letters are filled with references to his prayer for those whom he loves. 'God is my witness,' he writes to the Romans, 'that without ceasing I mention you always in my prayers' (Romans 1:9). It is as though on those journeys by land and sea the prayer of intercession was constantly and lovingly in his heart and even on his lips. This is a prayer which rises not from Paul's little ego but from Christ who lives in him. And as Paul prays for others, so he humbly asks the Colossians to pray for him. After all is it not a great art to receive the prayer of others? Just as we must learn to receive love, so we must learn to open our hearts gratefully to the loving prayers that others offer for us.

There are, of course, various levels of intercessory prayer. There is the almost casual prayer of one who intercedes for others because he has promised to do so. This is all right. But there is another form of intercession in which one becomes deeply involved with another person or with other persons. This is a prayer which may be accompanied by fasting and watching and suffering like that of Moses: 'Then I lay prostrate before the Lord as before, forty days and forty nights; I neither ate bread nor drank water . . . and I prayed for Aaron also at the same time' (Deuteronomy 9:18-20).

Such a prayer demands a going out from oneself, a forgetfulness of self (and forgetfulness of self is always an indispensable condition for enlightenment) and a total empathy with another person in whose place one stands. But (and here is the difficult thing) I cannot become attached to the person for whom I intercede. I must allow myself to be drawn up into God, leaving the person for whom I pray in order to find him or her again in God.

The process is beautifully described by a Russian *staretz* who describes his prayer for the workers who have been entrusted to him. He prays at first in a very concrete way for particular persons for whom he feels compassion:

> Lord, remember Nicholas, he is so young, he has left his newborn child to find work because they are so poor he has no other means of supporting it. Think of him and protect him from evil thoughts. Think of her and be her defender.   (Bloom, p. 14)

Here is a prayer of empathy, a prayer in which the *staretz* suffers with the people whom he loves. But as he perseveres he finds that he is drawn up into the cloud of unknowing. Just as the man in search of the ox finds that the ox disappears, so the holy *staretz* finds that Nicholas and his wife and child disappear. And not only them. Everything is forgotten and the *staretz* is alone, immersed in the silence of God:

> Thus I pray but as I feel the presence of God more and more strongly I reach a point where I can no longer take notice of anything on earth. The earth vanishes and God alone remains. Then I forget Nicholas, his wife, his child, his village, his poverty and am carried away in God. (Bloom, p. 14)

This loss of self corresponds to the big circle of nothingness where one forgets everything and is totally lost in the absolute. Wonderful prayer of intercession. *The Cloud of Unknowing* insists that by remaining in silent mystical prayer I am in fact helping the whole human race and the souls of the dead. I do not think explicitly of anybody, but I am helping everybody.

But this total forgetfulness is not the last step. Just as the wise old man returns to the market-place, so the *staretz* must return to Nicholas, his wife and his child. And so he writes:

> Then deep in God I find the divine love which contains Nicholas, his wife, his child, their poverty, their needs – this divine love is a torrent which carries me back to earth and to praying for them. And the same thing happens again. God's presence becomes stronger, earth recedes. I am carried again into the depths where I find the world God so greatly loves. (Bloom, p. 15)

And so in the last stage he sees through the eyes of God. Now it is God who loves through him; and this is unrestricted love which is unattached and liberated from craving.

III

It may happen that someone has a calling or vocation to intercessory prayer for another person or for other persons or for the world; and this prayer will consume his whole being and draw him up into the cloud of unknowing in the silent love I have described. Here he will be in the emptiness, the nothingness and the void, in a state of detachment from all thinking or reasoning or feeling; but his very being, his existential being, is an offering to God like the offering of Jesus on the Cross.

The Book of Privy Counselling speaks of such prayer and the author seems to regard it as the apex of the mystical life. He describes how, naked of self and clothed with Christ, one offers oneself to the Father with the words:

> That which I am and the way that I am with all my gifts of nature and grace you have given me, O Lord, and you are all this. I offer it to you principally to praise you and to help my fellow Christians and myself. (Johnston (1), ch. 3)

This is a remarkable prayer. It is existential: a total offering of one's being. 'You are all this' – in other words, God is my being and I am (as the author says elsewhere) worshipping God with himself. This is Trinitarian in that one offers oneself in Christ to the Father. Moreover, the offering is made for a threefold intention: to praise God, to help my fellow Christians, to help myself. How interesting that the prayer of intercession should reach its climax in praise – 'principally to praise you'!

The notion of sacrificing oneself in intercession is deeply embedded in human nature. It entered increasingly into the heart of Gandhi as his death drew near. All his life Gandhi had been aware of the power of suffering and non-violence and the Cross; but at the end he saw clearly that the most powerful force in the world was the offering of one's life in martyrdom. He became increasingly fascinated by the thought of Christ and his sacrifice. While in Rome we are told that he wept before the crucifix in the Sistine Chapel; and later, the only picture on the bare walls of his little room was that of Christ. Whereas the activist Gandhi had loved the prayer of Newman: 'Lead, kindly light,' the later Gandhi turned to the Christian hymn: 'When I survey the wondrous Cross.' Killed by the bullet of a fellow Hindu while walking to a prayer meeting, he died with the name of God on his lips: 'Ram, Ram!'

For all his faults (and he had plenty) Gandhi is for me a Christlike figure. He is one of those great religious personalities who becomes more and more universal, who takes upon himself the suffering of the human race, who offers himself to God for the salvation of the world. In this one sees the potential greatness of human nature.

IV

All that I have said leads to a vitally important conclusion; namely, that the greatest force in the world is not the conscious efforts of men and women who make plans, construct buildings, travel continents and change the face of the earth. All this is good and I would be the last person to oppose human progress. But there is another power at work in the universe and it is a power that can be tapped by men and women of faith. As I have said, Oriental religions speak of the life-force and of *karma*; Christians have always spoken of grace and faith and love. It is precisely here that there lies the power to move mountains and to shake the earth. This was the point of Jesus when he spoke of the widow who dropped her mite into the donation box. 'Truly, I say to you, this poor widow has put more than all those who are contributing to the treasury. For they contributed out of their abundance; but she out of her poverty has put in everything she had, her whole living' (Mark 12:43,44). Her mite contributed little; but her loving sacrifice – this shook the universe and the universe is still shaking under its impact.

This can be applied to social action. It is the cup of water given in the name of Jesus that counts. This principle was admitted by such a great activist as Gandhi. Tagore had given him the name of Mahatma, the great-souled; and Gandhi could reply: 'My Mahatmanship is worthless. It is due to my outward activities, due to my politics which is the least part of me and is therefore evanescent. What is of abiding worth is my insistence on truth, non-violence and Brahmacharya, which is the real part of me. That permanent part of me, however small, is not to be despised. It is my all' (Duncan, p. 166).

This is the Gandhi who insisted that his non-violence was a creed, not political expedience. Belief always creates something, even when we do not see tangible results. Some people have said that Gandhi failed – that he left India in a political and economic chaos from which it never recovered. Others have said that he was magnificently successful and changed the course of history. But in either case we must measure the achievement of Gandhi by his own standards – 'My Mahatmanship is worthless.' His faith and love, like that of the widow, gave birth to spiritual vibrations which will always remain.

The same can be said of Mother Teresa of Calcutta. Judged in terms of economics, she and her sisters have done little to alleviate the poverty of the Indian sub-continent. But their love and compassion generate a spiritual power which remains. Let me again quote her words:

> We can do very little for the people, but at least they know that we love them and that we care for them and that we are at their disposal. So let us try, all of us, to come closer to that unity of spreading Christ's love wherever we go, love and compassion; have deep compassion for the people.

This again is the power which shakes the universe.

Now while I emphasize the power of compassion and love and enlightenment, it is by no means my intention to downgrade human efficiency, plans for economic progress, political acumen and conscious effort. Far from it. The great challenge of our day is to unite these two forces. In other words, the great challenge of our day is mysticism in action. Our age demands not only men and women who will retire to caves in the Himalayas and huts in the desert to intercede for mankind but also men and women who will enjoy mystical experience in the hurly-burly of politics and economics and social action. The activity of such people will bear fruit because it is rooted in the Tao, rooted in non-action, rooted in God. In them human action falls into the stream of non-action and progress is made.

18. *Mysticism in Action*

Critics of mysticism frequently point to the immense social problems of our day – the hunger, the air pollution, the social injustice, the racial discrimination, the political corruption, the danger of nuclear war, the exploitation of the rich by the poor, the torture of political prisoners. And then they ask about mysticism. How will this help solve contemporary problems? Is it not a luxury to retire to the desert while large sections of humanity face utter destruction? Surely the first duty of modern man is to stretch out a helping hand to his fellow-men and women, to alleviate their suffering, to bring peace and happiness to the world.

These statements and these questions are all very reasonable. Of course we must marshal our forces to help suffering humanity and to build a better world. The only problem is: how? Activists sometimes overlook the undeniable fact that unenlightened, unregenerate, unconverted men and women can do nothing to solve the vast problems with which we are confronted. Not only will they do nothing but they may do immense damage. They may line their own pockets with the money which should go to the poor (and, alas, we have seen this happen very often); or they may be carried away by passionate anger and violently create more problems than they solve; or they may simply lack the depth and vision to see the roots of the problems. The weakness of human nature is something we cannot with impunity overlook. Buddhism teaches that prior to enlightenment we are in illusion – we are lost in the woods and don't even see the footprints of the ox. And then Christianity teaches about original sin. In either case, to work for humanity one must be enlightened. What the modern world needs is enlightened men and women.

Once enlightened we no longer rely on our little ego but on a power which is greater than ourselves. 'Apart from me,' says Jesus, 'you can do nothing' (John 15:5). And Paul, carried away to boast that he has laboured more than all the others, is forced to correct himself: 'it was not I, but the grace of God which is with me' (1 Corinthians 15:10). Yes, Paul. You never said a truer word. It was not your strength; it was a greater power within you to which you surrendered. Your strength was in weakness. Your action was rooted in non-action.

And so if we are in any way to solve the problems of our day we must rely on the power of another, not on our own power. And this is non-action which, I have tried to say, is the most powerful action of all. It manifests itself in the human heart as a blind stirring of love, as a living flame of love. Sometimes, it is true, this inner fire drives people into solitude where they intercede for mankind and unleash a power which shakes the universe. But the same inner fire drives others into the midst of action with a passionate love for justice and a willingness to die for their convictions. Indeed, this flame of love may suddenly become dynamic in the heart of a solitary – who suddenly discovers that he is called to action and that he cannot refuse the invitation. Such was the shepherd-prophet Amos who protests: 'I am no prophet, nor a prophet's son; but I am a herdsman, and a dresser of sycamore trees, and the Lord took me from following the flock, and the Lord said to me, "Go, prophesy to my people Israel" ' (Amos 7:14,15). Poor Amos! Like Jeremiah and Jonah he did not want to be involved in tumultuous action; but the inner flame, the inner voice, drove him on and, under its influence, he thundered against the rich:

> Hear this, you who trample upon the needy
> and bring the poor of the land to an end
> > (Amos 8:4)

Here is the action which is the overflow of mysticism. It is filled with compassion for the poor and needy and underprivileged.

II

I have said that the mystical flame sometimes drives hermits or solitaries into action. But I can immediately hear the objection: 'But the mystic who has spent long periods in solitude knows nothing about the world. How, then, can he solve its problems? Let him subscribe to *Time* and *Newsweek*. Let him read the *New York Times*. Or, better still, let him take a guided tour around Calcutta and be "exposed to the poor". Then we'll listen to him.'

Well, well. I wonder. Let us never underestimate the wisdom of the desert. For the fact is that the person who has spent long periods in authentic prayer and meditation knows about the suffering of the world because he has experienced it all within himself. How often has a repentant sinner, filled with remorse for his iniquities and failures, gone to the solitary monk to confess his crimes – and, lo and behold, he has found someone who understands the whole story. For the monk has experienced it all within himself – in another way. He has met the devil and seen his own awful weakness and potentiality for evil. It does not shock him to hear about murder and rape and violence – and he is filled with compassion for the weakness of a human race to which he himself belongs. Moreover, like Kannon who with that exquisite smile of compassion hears the cries of the poor, the mystic also has in his own way heard the cries of the underprivileged, the downtrodden, the victims of violence and deceit and exploitation – just as Jesus knew it all in Gethsemane. Of course it will do him no harm to read *Time* and *Newsweek* also. And if he does, he will find there things which the authors of the articles did not realize.

In the midst of solitude, then, a person may receive a prophetic vocation like that of Amos. And he may struggle against it. But his struggle will be in vain; and he will be pursued by the inexorable words: 'To all to whom I send you you shall go, and whatever I command you you shall speak. Be not afraid of them, for I am with you to deliver you, says the Lord' (Jeremiah 1:7). And so he goes into action and his action is fruitful because the Lord is with him and because he sees problems at their root and in their totality. His enlightened eye penetrates through the lines of *Time* and *Newsweek* to the basic cause of all our problems which is that mysterious reality which Christians call sin and Buddhists call blindness and ignorance.

I have spoken of the solitary who is called to action. But the mystic in action need not have been solitary. He may (and this is the Ignatian ideal) be a person who has spent his years in a cycle of contemplation-action-contemplation-action; and in this way he has attained to enlightenment. The important thing is not whether or not he has spent years in solitude. What matters is that he should be enlightened – that his eye of love penetrate beyond the superficial appearances to the root cause of our problems and to the ultimate solution which lies beyond the cloud of unknowing.

But what, you may ask, will he do? And to this I can only answer, as in my previous chapter, that he will follow the guidance of the inner light. Nor is this an easy task. Because following the light is different from following an idea or an ideology. It demands liberation from ideology so that one can listen to the voice of the beloved which will, at times, run counter to all ideologies. But one must discern that voice; and we find that the true mystic in action is always praying for light, always searching for the way. His initial call points out the general direction, but it does not enlighten every step of the path. Quite often there will be anguish and fear and uncertainty and conflict like that of Jeremiah: 'Woe is me, my mother, that you bore me, a man of strife and contention to the whole land!' (Jeremiah 15:10).

This inner light leads in the most surprising ways. Prophetical people are quite unpredictable. Often they are socially unacceptable, strident, exaggerated, apparently unorthodox. Like Jeremiah they are often ridiculed and put in the stocks. Usually they are put to death, either literally or metaphorically. But the distinctive thing is the quality of their love which 'bears all things, believes all things, hopes all things, endures all things' (1 Corinthians 13:7).

Consequently there is no blueprint to tell us what the mystic in action will do. He might do anything. But, on the other hand, he will have his charisma which he must faithfully follow. And this is true of all of us. We are not called to serve in the same way. 'Are all apostles? Are all prophets? Are all teachers? Do all work miracles? Do all possess gifts of healing? Do all speak with tongues? Do all interpret?' (1 Corinthians 12:29). We cannot ask that every prophet walk in peace marches or teach the blind or visit the sick or denounce the politically corrupt. Each must follow his own distinctive charisma.

And we must have our ears to the ground to listen for the true prophets, to recognize them, to follow their guidance and not to kill them. This is the great challenge of our day. Around us are prophets and false prophets. By their fruits we shall know them; by their fruits only can we distinguish the authentic from the pretenders. And Paul has spoken of those fruits of the Spirit which are 'love, joy, peace, patience, kindness, goodness, faithfulness, gentleness, self-control' (Galatians 5:22). If these are present we should listen to the prophet, even when his words run counter to what we hold sacred and believe.

III

St Paul says that the important thing is love. After extolling the various charismatic gifts he goes on to say that what is, or should be, common to them all is love. Without love the gifts are useless. And so he begins his canticle: 'If I speak in the tongues of men and of angels, but have not love, I am a noisy gong or a clanging cymbal' (1 Corinthians 13:1).

Gandhi recognized this; but in his peculiar circumstances he preferred to speak of non-violence or *ahimsa*. This included compassion for the poor, love of the aggressor, love of justice. It renounced all hatred and use of force; but it believed in force of another kind: *satyagraha* means the force of truth.

To build one's activity on love and non-violence demands the greatest inner purification. One must constantly rid one's heart of inordinate desires and fears and anxieties; but above all one must cleanse oneself from anger.

In our day anger seems to be the chief enemy of love and non-violence. By anger I mean the inner violence which lies not only in the conscious but also in the unconscious mind of individuals and of whole nations. This is an inner violence which has sometimes been nurtured by decades of oppression and injustice; sometimes it has been further nurtured by domestic strife in the home; always it is the source of great insecurity, inner fear and awful weakness. This is the anger which may erupt into sexual crimes or irrational murder and terrorism.

Now if I come to recognize the anger which is in me (and this is already great progress in the journey towards human maturity) and if I ask a psychologist what I am to do with my anger, the odds are that he will tell me, among other things, to get it out of my system. 'Get it out somehow! Imagine that your enemy is seated beside you and just roar at him – tell him what you feel! Or thump a pillow or a punch-ball or a sack of hay! But get it out!'

Now this may sound a thousand miles away from mystical experience. But in fact it is not. Because in the mystical path anger comes out – it rises to the surface of consciousness. Remember that I spoke of the Buddha sitting serenely in meditation while the beasts roar and the dogs bark. These are manifestations of my hidden anger. As I have already said, I must not make violent efforts to chase them away, neither must I enter into dialogue with them. I simply pay no attention to them – and in doing this I accept them. And then they vanish. In some cases, of course, it may also be necessary to speak about them to a friend or counsellor. But in any case I get them out of my system.

But when this is done, something still remains. And this is *just anger*. In other words, my anger has not been annihilated but has been purified. Now it is the anger of one who has seen, and still sees, real injustice in his own life and in that of others and refuses to countenance such evil. It is an anger which could be more properly called *love of justice* and is accompanied by a willingness to die in the cause of justice. In itself this is nothing other than a mystical experience. It is the living flame of love orientated towards action.

Such was the righteous indignation of the prophets. Such was the anger of one who made a whip and drove the money-changers out of the temple: 'Take these things away; you shall not make my Father's house a house of trade' (John 2:16). Gandhi, too, was moved by this just anger: he spoke frequently of marshalling all one's spiritual forces against the oppressor and he fought injustice by fasting, by suffering, by accepting imprisonment and by non-violence.

IV

From all that has been said and from a perusal of the Fourth Gospel it will be clear that mystical action is chiefly a matter of bearing fruit. It is not a question of frenetic activity, of getting a lot done, of achieving immediate results. Rather is it a question of unrestricted love which goes on and on and on.

Such love always bears fruit. Such love always leads to a union which creates something new. But the new creation may be quite different from what the mystic and his followers expected. His life, like that of Jesus, may end in apparent failure. But when it does, people in another part of the world and perhaps in another era will reap the fruit. For 'here the saying holds true, "One sows and another reaps". I sent you to reap that for which you did not labour; others have laboured and you have entered into their labour' (John 4:37,38).

19. *Training for Mysticism (1)*

I

Throughout this book I have stressed the fact that mysticism is the gift of God and the work of grace. And yet it is also true that the great religious traditions have used human means to educate people and introduce them to mysticism. How these two factors, divine grace and human effort, are theologically reconciled need not concern us here. Enough to say that monastic life, whether Christian or Buddhist, has always attempted through training and discipline to educate the contemplative faculties which exist in all men and women and which are of particular importance for those who would devote themselves to meditation and prayer. Such contemplative faculties concern that realm which we call 'the heart' but they are also deeply embedded in the body; and in Asia there has always been particular skill in educating and forming a contemplative body. These faculties, however, have become blunted in modern life by the tremendous bombardment to which our senses have been exposed. Consequently, modern people are looking for a new spirituality and a new asceticism which will enable them to benefit from the good points of scientific progress while at the same time developing and training those mystical faculties which lead to enlightenment. This is quite a challenge.

In the Sino-Japanese tradition spiritual training is called *gyo* and is represented by the character which means going and walking and which originally pictured a road or a crossroads (See overleaf) This character translates the Sanskrit *carya* and is defined in a standard Buddhist dictionary as: 'Religious acts, deeds or exercises aimed at taking one closer to the final goal of enlightenment.'[1] In other words, as the very core of Buddhism is the awakening or enlightenment so *gyo* includes anything that carries one along the way to this goal.

Buddhist monasticism contains a very elaborate and meticulous *gyo* which gives instructions on how to walk, how to sit, how to dress how to eat, how to fast, how to sleep, how to breathe, how to bathe

[1] *Japanese-English Buddhist Dictionary* (Daito Shuppansha: Tokyo 1965, p. 93).

(*By kind permission of Kakichi Kadowaki*)

how to train the body and make it flexible, how to develop vital energy, how to be authentically detached, how to act in time of sickness. It also gives instructions on certain ascetical practices such as running around the mountain (I speak here of Mount Hiei) for days or weeks, sitting for long periods in the lotus posture, reciting the sutras, copying the sutras, bowing and touching the ground with one's forehead, prostrations, striking the gong while reciting the name of Amida – and so on, and so on.

Naturally enough, this *gyo* has had its difficulties and its critics. As happened in similar circumstances in the West, it often deteriorated into an external legalism which simply put burdens on people without bringing them to the coveted goal of enlightenment. And so we find the saintly Japanese monk Shinran (1173–1263) rebelling against the asceticism of the Tendai and Zen sects and proclaiming the pre-eminence of faith and of grace. Shinran himself had spent much time practising *gyo* on Mount Hiei near Kyoto and

had profited little from it all. And so he proclaimed faith in Amida
as the one means of salvation. Everything is gift, he declared;
everything is grace: one drop of the mercy of Amida is of more value
than all the *gyo* in the wide world. He was the first Japanese Buddhist
monk openly to abandon celibacy and to take a wife – for celibacy
was part of the *gyo* which he rejected. He has frequently been compared to Luther, all the more so since he preached a doctrine which
appealed not only to monks but to ordinary working persons who
had neither the time nor the capacity for the prolonged austerities
of Tendai and Zen. Simply call on the name of Amida with faith –
this was his message. Recite the name of Amida (and this was called
the *nembutsu*) and you will be reborn in the Pure Land which lies to
the West.

Shinran preached the doctrine of reliance on another (*tariki*) as
opposed to the self-reliance (*jiriki*) of Zen. While Zen proclaimed
the difficult *gyo* (*nan-gyo*), Shinran and his followers proclaimed the
easy *gyo* (*i-gyo*) as the way to salvation. Yet in practice his path is
not so easy. The very renunciation of asceticism is a *gyo* in itself.
It demands a total detachment.

II

In the Christian tradition, too, there has been training and education
for enlightenment and conversion. St Ignatius speaks of 'spiritual
exercises' (and this might be the best translation of the word *gyo*)
and he describes these exercises: 'For just as taking a walk, journeying
on foot, and running are bodily exercises, so we call spiritual exercises every way of preparing and disposing the soul to rid itself of all
inordinate attachments, and, after their removal, of seeking and
finding the will of God in the disposition of our life for the salvation
of our soul' (Ignatius (1), p. 1). Here is an interesting parallel to
Buddhism: detachment leading to enlightenment or conversion and
salvation. For Ignatius this conversion entails the discovery of
God's will.

Ignatius, of course, is appealing to an ancient tradition in which
asceticism is associated with the Hellenistic games just as Buddhist
gyo is associated with the martial arts like judo, karate, fencing and
wrestling. St Paul refers to the sports of his day:

Do you not know that in a race all the runners compete, but only
one receives the prize? So run that you may obtain it. Every

athlete exercises self-control in all things. They do it to receive a perishable wreath, but we an imperishable. (1 Corinthians 9:24,25)

The thought of the games is often in Paul's mind – Paul who is running towards the goal without looking back, Paul who has fought the good fight, who has finished the course, who has kept the faith.

As the art of asceticism developed, the old authors began to speak of interior and exterior asceticism. The orthodox teaching was that the exterior, which included fasting, watching, observance of silence and discipline of all kinds, was only of value in so far as it led to the interior which meant love of neighbour, compassion for the suffering, humility and simplicity of life.

And yet in Christianity, as in Buddhism, wise people were always acutely aware of the dangers of asceticism and of minute fidelity to law. For one thing they realized that the exterior could be over-emphasized to the detriment of the interior, thus leading to pride, self-centredness and the building up of the very egoism it was meant to destroy. Indeed, the prophets of the Old Testament had kept insisting that Yahweh wants our hearts rather than our sacrifices: rend your hearts and not your garments. This is particularly stressed in Isaiah:

Is not this the fast that I choose . . . Is it not to share your bread with the hungry, and bring the homeless poor into your house; and when you see the naked, to cover him, and not to hide yourself from your own flesh? 　　　　　　　　(Isaiah 58:6,7)

This is also a central theme in the Gospel: the observance of the sabbath, the washing of hands, fasting and all kinds of external observance are subordinate to justice and truth and charity. And is not this a theme that must always be replayed? Because the dangers of legalism are perennial.

And so in East and West we find the same tension. On the one hand, some training or education is necessary; on the other hand, all depends on grace. On the one hand, we must strive; on the other hand, our striving is itself a gift. On the one hand, asceticism is necessary; on the other hand, it is spiritually dangerous. In practice the problem has been solved by a principle which states that we should strive with our human abilities as though all depended on ourselves, and yet we must wait for the gift as though all depended on God.

III

In our own day the Western wave of interest in meditation and mysticism brings with it a great interest in asceticism. Modern practical people want to know *how to do it*. They want to be shown the way. And so their eyes turn towards the *gyo* of the East – towards the foothills of the Himalayas and the temples of Kyoto. Who will give me a methodology, a spirituality, a system? Where will I find a master?

And while these questions are asked, thinking people are also acutely aware of the grave defects and failures of the asceticism of the past. Apart from the dangers which I have already mentioned and which are stressed in the Gospel, there is the additional voice of protest from many people who have gone through the training and found it ineffective – even counter-productive. They faithfully observed all the rules of a religious or monastic system; but the whole thing did not touch their innermost being, did not penetrate beyond the surface. It all remained external; and they did not even reach the threshold of contemplation. This is a complaint which one hears from Christians and Buddhists alike. Why was the law never internalized? What was wrong?

Again, an objection raised in the West is that the traditional asceticism has paid little attention to the training of human feeling and affectivity. Modern people are peculiarly sensitive to this, since they live in a culture which has rediscovered the beauty of matter, of feeling, of sexuality. Read Teilhard de Chardin on *The Evolution of Chastity* and you find a powerful statement of the inadequacy of the old approach which frequently warped and crushed that human feeling which should blossom and bloom through the message of the Gospel.

Now it seems to me that we will not find a new asceticism or spirituality simply by delving into the past of either Buddhism or Christianity. This is an area in which, recalling that religions are evolving, we must turn to dialogue between the great religions and their common dialogue with modern psychology and culture. Furthermore, this is an area in which we will not get instantaneous results, for neither psychology nor religion can claim an adequate understanding of human feeling and human sexuality. We have a long way to go; and a great challenge lies before us. Let me, then, mention a few points which are no more than guide-lines; and then in the next chapter I will select some aspects of Buddhist *gyo* which may be of interest to modern people.

IV

First of all let me say that if the old asceticism failed in many ways this was principally due to a lack of love. The trouble with the Pharisees was not that they kept all the rules (their observance was praiseworthy) but that they did not love enough. And that is why their rules remained external. Similarly, in any ascetical training the only thing which will internalize the outer observance of the law is love – that human and religious love which is unrestricted, which goes on and on and on. That is why I have spoken about the interior law of charity and of love which is above all laws and rules and observances. That is why I have spoken of the living flame of love, the blind stirring of love, the small fire and the murmuring stream.

And it should be remembered that this love must be directed to ourselves. Love of self is important. Though this is proclaimed in Deuteronomy and reiterated even more strongly in the Gospel, it has been a weak point of traditional asceticism. It is so easy to fall into a holy self-hatred, as it was sometimes called; it is so easy to fall into a morbid delight in doing the difficult thing. And it has taken modern psychology to remind us that we must love ourselves, accept ourselves, listen to ourselves, trust our deepest feelings and instincts. Only in this context can austerity be holy and enriching.

Again, there is love of God, love of the Gospel, love of the community. Buddhists texts, as I have frequently said, do not make much of love and do not talk about love. But this does not mean that love and commitment are absent. It is interesting to recall that Buddhist temples everywhere resound with an archetypal invocation which is the very essence of their religious practice:

> I take refuge in the Buddha
> I take refuge in the *dharma* (the law)
> I take refuge in the *sangha* (the community)

Here is total commitment to what is called the triple jewel. Is this not an expression of love? And is it not interesting to see the very personal nature of the first invocation, the dedication of oneself to Shakamuni, the enlightened one?

I said that the triple invocation is archetypal. And, of course, the corresponding Christian commitment could be expressed in the words:

> I take refuge in Jesus
> I take refuge in the Gospel
> I take refuge in the Church

Here is a great love, an unrestricted love for the whole universe and for its source. When *gyo* is practised in this setting and when it leads to such commitment it cannot but be human, it cannot but be internalized.

Put in other words, faith is the very core and essence from which all asceticism flows and to which it returns. Buddhist faith develops into total commitment to the Buddha, to the *dharma*, to the *sangha*. Christian faith develops into total commitment to Jesus, to the Gospel, to the Church. Both, I believe, move on to faith in the great mystery which lies beyond the Buddha, the *dharma*, the *sangha* – to the great mystery which lies beyond Jesus, the Gospel, the Church. This is the great mystery which Christians call God our Father and the Father of Our Lord Jesus Christ.

I have spoken of the *sangha* and the Church. This recalls the vitally important fact that we cannot practise asceticism and meditation alone; we cannot arrive at mysticism alone. Just as Paul had to go to Ananias to receive the imposition of hands after his initial encounter with Jesus on the road to Damascus, so we also need other people. We need people whom we love and by whom we are loved; we need a climate of trust and of union. Only in such a community can mysticism develop – 'if we love one another, God abides in us and his love is perfected in us' (1 John 4:12).

Obviously this does not mean that we must live under the same roof with the whole community. It simply means that we must be united with them even when distance or the need for solitude separate us physically. Ordinarily Christians are united with a small group and through it with the whole Church and the human race; Buddhists are united with their *dharma* brothers and sisters, then with the whole *sangha* and then with the universe.

As for the precise nature of the smaller community which leads to mysticism, I would not restrict myself to one format. There are innumerable possibilities.

The traditional type of community in Christianity and Buddhism alike tends towards monasticism. It centres around a master who guides his disciples to enlightenment, to conversion, to mysticism. Such a master reads the Scriptures and comments on them – not in the scholarly fashion of the exegete but in the enlightened manner of one whose inner eye of love sees in the Scriptures treasures which are hidden from the wise and prudent. Again, he explains the *dharma* or the Gospel. He interviews his disciples one by one, enjoying with them the religious experience about which I have spoken in this book. Sometimes this religious experience will be expressed in words but at other times words will be unnecessary – the two can remain in silent and communal contemplation. In this way the teacher mediates the God experience; he brings the disciple to enlightenment. Indeed, enlightenment (sudden or gradual) may take place precisely during this interview.

Yet this meeting has a profoundly human dimension also. A story is told that when Ignatius (who was one of the great directors of Western Christianity) saw that one of his disciples was glum and downcast he danced a Spanish tango to cheer him up. When one reflects on the game leg of Ignatius, the legacy of Pamplona, one can imagine that the disciple quickly snapped out of his desolation.

Master and disciples form one kind of community. But it is only one. There are, as I have said, other possibilities. The founders of the religious orders had different ideas about the nature of community – some advocating stability, others advocating constant travel on the road. Again, in our day and before our eyes new forms of community are emerging. There are charismatic communities in which each member has his or her special gift. 'To each is given the manifestation of the Spirit for the common good' (1 Corinthians 1:7). In such a community, as Paul says, some will teach, others will speak in prophecy, others will interpret, others will heal. What matters is that they love and trust one another and in this way cultivate a soil in which authentic mysticism can grow and develop.

I would not, then, limit community to one particular format. This is an area in which modern people are searching; and it is scarcely possible to imagine the form which communities will take in the decades which lie ahead.

20. *Training for Mysticism (2)*

I

I have indicated that Buddhist *gyo* or asceticism is extremely meticulous and extends to every area of human activity. Consequently I cannot treat it here in detail but must content myself with outlining a few general principles which may be useful for my reader in his or her quest for enlightenment.

But first let me recall that the Buddhist asceticism found in Japan owes a great debt to Taoism and the whole stream of Sino-Japanese culture – and it is about this that I will principally speak. To understand it one must to some extent grasp its peculiar approach to the human body, an approach which is quite different from the Hellenistic body-and-soul way of thinking that became traditional in the West. The East Asian approach is found pre-eminently in Oriental medicine – in acupuncture, moxibustion, and the many forms of massage. It is also in evidence in the martial arts like karate, judo, aikido and sumo; and even in the fine arts like the tea ceremony and the flower arrangement.

In all these activities the centre of gravity is not the head but the belly or *hara*. (It is interesting to note, in parenthesis, that in the *yin-yang* scheme of things the belly is *yin*. That is to say, it is feminine; and in this sense contemplation, as envisaged by Chinese philosophy, is a feminine activity.) And particular attention is paid to the area which lies a couple of inches below the navel. This is called the *tanden* or *kikai*, the latter word meaning literally 'the sea of energy'.

When I use the word energy I am thinking of the Japanese *ki* (pronounced like the English *key*), the Chinese *chi* and the Sanskrit *prana*. All these words point to a certain cosmic energy or vital force which courses through the whole universe, linking all things together, and courses also through the human body when it is healthy. One who possesses a wealth of *ki* can perform extraordinary feats; and yet it differs from muscular energy in that it nourishes spiritual activities like meditation and, according to some, reaches its peak at the moment of death when physical strength is ebbing away.

And yet *ki* heals. One can learn to direct it to the affected part of the body, thus healing oneself. Or by imposing hands on another one can allow the *ki* to flow through one's body into the body of another, thus imparting healing and strength. Indeed, the Japanese word for healing is *teate* literally meaning 'imposition of hands'; and in the ancient Oriental world people healed others by laying their hands on them.[1]

Closely associated with this *ki* is another concept which has already appeared in my book; namely, *muga* meaning non-self or *mushin* no-mind. This is the art of losing self, emptying one's mind, entering into a state of relaxed awareness. This emptiness is, it should be noted, a state of profound concentration in which the mind is liberated not only from reasoning and thinking but also from hatred and passion and fear, so that a great calm descends upon the person. Losing oneself in this way, one can 'become the object', whether that object be a flower or a bow or a flowing stream.

Only in this state of no-mind will the *ki* flow through one's body; and only in this state of no-mind can one impart healing to another. For the *ki* is blocked by tension or anxiety or hatred or rancour of any kind.

A good Oriental master is aware of his own *ki* and he can, so to speak, catch the *ki* of his disciple. He can learn very much by observing the eyes, the throat, the breathing. Sometimes he has a gaze which is embarrassingly piercing and penetrating. All this is part of his process of discernment.

But remember that this *gyo* is, to to speak, neutral. Obviously it is very good to lose one's self in order to be filled with the Holy Spirit. It is also good to lose self so that the inner creative and artistic powers may surface. It is also healthy when one is trained to lose self in sports like judo. But the non-self state can also be dangerous. In some forms of ecstatic religion one empties the mind in order to allow a spirit to take over or in order to enter into a frenzy. For this reason an authentic master teaches his disciple to enter into emptiness with great discipline and purity of intention. For *muga* and

---

[1] Scientific studies have been made on this *ki* or vital energy; but modern physics is not yet prepared to assert that it exists. It is possible that we have here a phenomenon which does not fall under the aegis of science and does not obey the laws of physics as we know them. Some people claim that an understanding of *ki* would throw light on parapsychological phenomena like telepathy, clairvoyance and thought projection.

mushin and *ki* are not things to be treated lightly. They are very serious.

But now, keeping in mind these fundamental concepts, and also keeping in mind what I said in the last chapter about the supreme importance of faith and love, let me consider three aspects of Buddhist ascetical training: *control of the mind, control of the breathing, control of the body.* These three approaches converge at the desired goal of heightened awareness and even, under certain circumstances, at enlightenment.

II

First, then, is control of the mind. Eastern thought stresses what we all know from experience: that the human mind is restless, untamed, undisciplined like the wind. We constantly think of the future either with expectation or with apprehension; or we think of the past with nostalgia or with guilt. Seldom do we live in the present moment; seldom do we live in the here-and-now. We are always escaping from what we are and from what is.

Now the East has developed certain techniques for controlling the mind and bringing it to a standstill. And central among these is the art of concentrating on a single object so that the mind enters a state of one-pointedness.[1]

Concretely, one can concentrate on a part of the body – the space between the eyebrows, the tip of the nose, the lower abdomen. Or one can concentrate on a single thought. Or, as in Zen, one can concentrate on a *koan* or riddle. Or one can repeat a single sound or sacred word. Or one can become aware of the breathing. In all these cases one is concentrating on a single thing and, in consequence, becoming interiorly unified so as to enter the *mu-shin* or no-mind state about which I have spoken.

Or one can listen not to one sound but to every sound – a practice about which I spoke earlier in this book. Or one can watch every object that enters one's field of vision. And in this way one becomes totally aware of present reality.

Presence to each moment is a great ideal in Buddhist *gyo*; and

[1] *One-pointedness* seems to be the best translation of the Sanskrit *ekagrata* ('on a single point') and the Japanese *seishin toitsu* ('unification of spirit').

there is an old saying that 'a saint is one who walks when he walks, who talks when he talks, who does not dream while listening, who does not think while acting'. And, as I have said, a similar attentiveness is found in the arts. A teacher of calligraphy once told me that he can immediately tell from the ideographs where the writer lost one-pointedness and became distracted. His lapse affected his brush and appears in the writing.

Never underestimate one-pointedness. It gives remarkable power. It is the key to controlling the psychic energy or *ki* about which I have spoken; it is the key to influencing (and, alas, sometimes to manipulating) other people. I know a young Japanese man who can smash a heap of tiles with his forehead; and this he attributes to one-pointedness through the breathing. I myself believe that the secret of many feats, like those of the Fiji fire-walkers (whom I watched in Suva) or the yogis who pierce their cheeks with skewers, can be traced to this same one-pointedness. For in this state a latent dynamism of the human psyche is brought to the surface and people experience great power. If Asia has been labelled 'the mystic East' this is partly because Westerners have unconsciously adverted to the prevalence of one-pointedness in its life and culture.

Though one-pointedness is so central to all Asian culture, it is little known in the West outside the religious and mystical tradition. That is why transcendental meditation, which is a form of one-pointedness, has made such an impact. It has brought a new dimension into Western culture and has introduced many Westerners to a dynamism hitherto latent in their psyche. By taking a comfortable position and quietly repeating a mantra one comes to the deeper level of consciousness where one-pointedness resides. This gives relaxation, joy and renewed strength. It is interesting to note that transcendental meditation has made almost no impact in Japan nor even in India, its country of origin. No doubt this is because these countries already possess one-pointedness in their culture. Transcendental meditation offers nothing new.

One-pointedness looks very like mysticism. But do not be deceived! It is here that one must use discernment. For mysticism (and please forgive me for repeating it again) is centred on faith whereas profound one-pointedness can be achieved without any faith whatever. It can be practised in a purely secular situation in order to develop human potential and ability to play ping-pong or golf. It can be used for good or evil, to heal or to destroy – a grim fact which is well known in Japan.

Zen masters distinguish clearly between those who sit in the lotus to develop human potential or to improve their karate and those who sit with faith, committing themselves totally and unconditionally to the Buddha, the *dharma* and the *sangha*. That is why an authentic master will quickly ask you what you want in your practice. And he will direct you accordingly.

A Christian example of one-pointedness is Mary Magdalen sitting at the feet of Jesus. 'One thing is needful' (Luke 10:42). Or again, Jesus tells us to live in the present without anxiety about the future. And here again the dimension of faith is stressed: 'Your heavenly Father knows that you need them all' (Matthew 6:32).

In general it can be said that mysticism is a form of one-pointedness; but not all one-pointedness is mysticism.

III

The second point was control of the breathing.

In all forms of Oriental meditation the breathing is of cardinal importance. Western medicine will agree that deep abdominal breathing is health-giving and invigorating; and Oriental thought adds to this the belief that breath or air is the principal source of life-giving *prana* or *ki* or cosmic energy. In yoga there are many breathing exercises and techniques; but in Buddhist meditation one just breathes naturally without in any way interfering with the inhalation or exhalation and without retention of breath. If one keeps the back straight, the breathing automatically becomes abdominal; and the aim in Buddhist asceticism is simply *to become aware of the breath.* This is called mindfulness (I referred to it earlier in this book) and it can be achieved first by counting the breath and then becoming aware of the breath without using any words. One may be aware of the breath at the nostrils, or of the rise and fall of the abdomen until eventually, one becomes aware of one's whole body. 'The wise man breathes from his heels' says an old Chinese proverb; and this well explains the awareness of the breath or the *ki* which flows through the body in this kind of meditation. Here is an ancient Buddhist text which describes mindfulness through the breathing:

A monk who has gone to a forest or the root of a tree or to an empty place, sits down cross-legged, holding his back erect, and arouses mindfulness in front of him. Mindful he breathes in, mindful he breathes out. Whether he is breathing in a long or a short breath, he comprehends that he is breathing in a long or a short breath. Similarly when he is breathing out. He trains himself, thinking: 'I shall breathe in, I shall breathe out, clearly perceiving the whole body'. (Conze, p. 56)

In this way the monk becomes aware of the vital energy and enters into one-pointedness.

The breath is of crucial importance because it gives access to the deeper levels of the psyche which are ordinarily unconscious. If we have a voluntary and involuntary nervous system, the former governing actions which can readily be controlled and the latter governing the inner functions like digestion which are normally outside of our control – if we look at the body in this way, then breathing stands between these two. Ordinarily it is involuntary; but it can easily be controlled and made rhythmical. And once one has learned to control the breathing, control of the remaining areas of the involuntary nervous system may follow. That is why the skilled yogi can control his digestion, his sleep and even his heartbeat. That is why he can penetrate to deep states of consciousness. 'By making his respiration rhythmical and progressively slower,' writes Mircea Eliade, 'the yogin can penetrate – that is, he can experience, in perfect lucidity – certain states of consciousness that are inaccessible in a waking condition, particularly the states of consciousness that are peculiar to sleep' (Eliade, p. 56).

Another important aspect of the breath is the fact that it symbolizes life – 'Then the Lord God formed man of dust from the ground, and breathed into his nostrils the breath of life' (Genesis 2:7). When I am breathing mindfully I become aware of the life within me; I become aware of my body; I become aware of the core of my being. I am reminded of the words of Jesus: 'Is not life more than food, and the body more than clothing?' (Matthew 6:25). How true! It is life that counts: the breath and the body. Other things like food and clothing are secondary.

Moreover in all the great religious traditions breath symbolizes something cosmic. *Ki* and *prana* have a cosmic dimension; and that is why they are associated with telepathy and thought-projection and the rest. Again, in the Hebrew-Christian tradition breath or *spiratio* symbolizes the Holy Spirit who fills the whole universe, who envelops us with his presence, who dwells within us. It is a wonderful fact of experience that, in those who have faith, mindfulness of the breathing can lead to a relishing of the presence of the Spirit. Some people's meditation consists in just breathing silently and wordlessly in the Spirit.

IV

The third point is control of the body.

There is a form of Buddhist meditation in which one becomes totally aware of one's body – it is a variation of the mindfulness about which I have already spoken. One simply sits on a chair (though in ancient times the cross-legged position was always used) with back erect, eyes closed, hands on thighs; and one experiences or feels the sensations of the body. The touch of the clothes on one's shoulders, the back pressing against the chair, the hips, the hands, the thighs, the soles of the feet. One does not *think about* the body: one *experiences* the body – moving one's awareness from one part of the body to the other until a profound relaxation is attained to. Here again the *ki* or vital energy courses through one's whole being.

But what, you may say, has this to do with religion, this body awareness? And to this I would answer that one passes through the body to the spirit. The same is true also of *hatha yoga* which is not just a form of physical training but a way to union – union with oneself and union with God. Some authors speak of a mysticism of posture; and while I do not accept this use of the word mysticism I sympathize with the underlying idea.

While there are many bodily postures in Oriental meditation, pride of place is given to the lotus. It is the perfect posture. With the left leg on the right thigh and the right foot on the left thigh, the back straight, the chin in, the strength in the abdomen – this posture brings one into silence and one-pointedness.

Sitting in the lotus is an art and an accomplishment. It is not mastered in one day but takes years of assiduous practice. One may, of course, learn the physical posture in a short time. But sitting in the lotus means more than this: it means that the stream of consciousness and the stream of the unconscious are brought to a standstill. One is 'just sitting', grasping the present moment in its totality, transcending time, liberated from anxiety and fear about future or past. This in itself is enlightenment.

When the bodily posture is correct one is enlightened. *The posture is the enlightenment.* That is why Suzuki Shunryu can write: 'When you have this posture, you have the right state of mind, so there is no need to try to attain some special state' (Suzuki, p. 22). Since mind and body are two sides of one coin, perfect bodily posture brings spiritual enlightenment.

V

Finally, et me recall that all the great mystical traditions speak of extraord·1ary psychic powers which may, or may not, appear in the course of the mystical journey. Such powers, alas, have caught the imagination of modern people, many of whom identify mysticism with telepathy, clairvoyance, out-of-the-body experience, thought projection, psychic auras and the like. Yet it is a mistake to pay too much attention to these things. They are no more than side-effects or by-products. What matters is faith and love.

Yoga speaks of *siddhis* or miraculous powers. These include the ability to read hearts, to see the future, to see things that are happening at distance. Others, which are less authenticated and the existence of which I question, are the ability to walk on water, to travel through the air, to pass through solid matter.

In yoga the appearance of psychic powers is significant in that it tells the master that his disciple is making progress. Yet no authentic master will encourage a disciple to seek such powers. Indeed, one must be wary of them because of the danger of vanity or what moderns might call 'inflation'. Moreover, there is the danger that, fascinated by the allure of power, one may be distracted from the principal goal which is salvation, total liberation, *moksa*.

Zen is even more radical in its rejection of extraordinary powers. The *mu . . . mu* about which I have spoken includes a rejection of any extraordinary power which may arise in the course of one's practice. All such things are treated as illusions like the *makyo* or 'world of the devil' through which one must pass on the way to enlightenment.

As for St John of the Cross, his attitude is somewhat similar. The nothing or *nada* which runs through his work entails a renunciation of clinging to all things, including psychic powers and supernatural gifts. Yet he sometimes speaks positively about enhanced vision as when he observes that 'the Holy Spirit illumines such souls . . . in many . . . present or future matters and about many events, even distant ones' (*Ascent*, 3:2,12). Here he attributes this knowledge to the Holy Spirit; but elsewhere he speaks of a natural cause:

> We affirm that those who have reached perfection or are already close to it, *usually* do possess light and knowledge about events happening in their presence and absence. *This knowledge derives from their illumined and purified spirits.* (*Ascent*, 2:26,13)

It is as though the body is spiritualized or sensitized in such a way that one's faculties penetrate beyond time and space and into the hearts of others. 'It is worthy of note,' he writes, 'that those *whose spirit is purified* can naturally perceive – some more than others – the inclinations and talents of men and what lies in the heart of the interior spirit. They derive this knowledge through exterior indications (even though extremely slight) such as words, gestures and other signs' (*Ascent*, 2:24,14).

Even though such knowledge may carry remarkable conviction, the Spanish mystic is always wary of it. It is not necessary; it may be a source of illusion. What matters is faith, naked faith, dark faith, the inner eye of love.

In a slightly different context St Paul speaks about charismatic gifts. He says that they are good in themselves but without love they are useless. 'If I speak in the tongues of men and angels, but have not love, I am a noisy gong or a clanging cymbal . . . And if I have prophetic powers, and understand all mysteries and all knowledge, and if I have all faith, so as to remove mountains, but have not love, I am nothing' (1 Corinthians 13:1,2). And the same can be said of psychic powers or enhanced vision. All these things are good in themselves but without love they are nothing.

And so I conclude where I began, recalling that mysticism is a question of love, a love which arises in the heart in answer to a call, a love which leads through the darkness of the cloud of unknowing to the great mystery which is light in itself but darkness to us. In East and West and in all the great religions, we find men and women who are in love without restriction and who look upon the world with eyes of love and compassion. Most of them are little known or talked about. Yet as long as such people walk the earth we can have unshakeable confidence in the future.

Books and articles quoted in the text

Abbot, Walter M. (editor): *The Documents of Vatican II* (Guild Press, New York, 1966).

Bloom, Anthony: *Courage to Pray* (Paulist Press, New York, 1973).

Butler, Edward Cuthbert: *Western Mysticism* (E. P. Dutton, New York, 1923).

Conze, Edward (editor): *Buddhist Texts* (Harper Torchbooks, New York, 1964).

Duncan, Ronald (editor): *Selected Writings of Mahatma Gandhi* (Fontana, London, 1971).

Eliade, Mircea (1): *The Two and the One* (Harper and Row, New York, 1965).

Eliade, Mircea (2): *Yoga: Immortality and Freedom* (Princeton University Press, New York, 1969).

French, R. M. (translator): *The Way of a Pilgrim* (The Seabury Press, New York, 1970).

Griffiths, Bede (1): *Christ in India* (Charles Scribner, New York, 1966).

Griffiths, Bede (2): *Return to the Centre* (Collins, London, 1976).

Heiler, Friedrich: *Prayer* (Oxford University Press, New York, 1958).

Ignatius of Loyola, St (1): *The Spiritual Exercises of St Ignatius*, Louis J. Puhl (editor), (Loyola University Press, Chicago, 1951).

Ignatius of Loyola, St (2): *St Ignatius' Own Story*, William Young (translator) (Regenery, Chicago, 1956).

Inge, William Ralph: *Christian Mysticism* (Methuen and Co, London, 1899).

James, William: *The Varieties of Religious Experience* (The Modern Library, New York, 1929).

John of the Cross, St: *The Collected Works of St John of the Cross*, translated by Kieran Kavanaugh, OCD, and Otilo Rodriguez, OCD (Institute of Carmelite Studies, Washington, DC).

Johnston, William (editor) (1): *The Cloud of Unknowing and The Book of Privy Counselling* (Doubleday, New York, 1973).

Johnston, William (2): *The Mysticism of 'The Cloud of Unknowing'* (Abbey Press, St Meinrad, Indiana, 1975).

Johnston, William (3): *Silent Music* (Collins, London, 1974 and Harper and Row, New York, 1974).

Johnston, William (4): *The Still Point* (Fordham University Press, New York, 1970).

Kadloubovsky, E. and Palmer, G. (translators): *Writings from the Philokalia* (Faber and Faber, London, 1967).

Lonergan, Bernard (1): *Method in Theology* (Darton, Longman and Todd, London, 1972).

Lonergan, Bernard (2): *A Second Collection* (Darton, Longman and Todd, London, 1974).

McDougall, A. (editor): *Spiritual Direction of Louis Lallement* (Newman, Westminster, 1946).

McKenzie, John L.: *Dictionary of the Bible* (Macmillan, New York, 1965).

Rogers, Carl: *On Becoming a Person* (Houghton Mifflin Co, Boston, 1961).

Shibayama, Zenkei: *Zen Comments on the Mumonkan* (Harper and Row, New York, 1974).

Suzuki, Shunryu *Zen Mind, Beginner's Mind* (Weatherhill, New York, 1970).

Tanquerey, Adolphe: *The Spiritual Life: A Treatise on Ascetical and Mystical Theology* (Newman, Westminster, 1947).

Teresa, Mother: 'The Poor in Our Midst' in *New Covenant* (Ann Arbor, Michigan, January, 1977).

Valera, J. Eduardo Perez: 'Toward a Transcultural Philosophy' in *Monumenta Nipponica*, volume XXVII (Tokyo, 1972).

Waldenfels, Hans: 'Absolute Nothingness' in *Monumenta Nipponica*, volume XXI (Tokyo, 1966).

Ware, Timothy (editor): *The Art of Prayer: An Orthodox Anthology*, compiled by Igumen Chariton of Valemo (Faber and Faber, London, 1966).

Woodward, F. L.: *The Minor Anthologies of the Pali Canons* (Oxford University Press, London, 1948).

Index

discernment (*contd.*)
163; evolution of, 163–4; New Testament roots, 160, 161
doctrines, formulation of, 81–2, 85
Dogen, 44, 143
Dominican mystics, Rhineland, 21, 45, 115
drama, 81
dryness, 36, 37, 38, 49, 127

Eckhart, Meister, 21, 120
ecstacies, 30
ego, 32, 109, 110
Eiheiji Temple, 110
Eleusinian mysteries, 16
Eliade, Mircea, 72, 72n, 192
Elijah, 37, 89
Eliot, T. S., 137
Elizabeth II, Queen, 109
emptiness, 10, 35, 66, 102, 103, 127; and compassion, 114; experience of God in, 121, 123; and growth of mystical love, 139; and *kenosis* of Jesus, 119; in Oriental mysticism, 106, 110–11; in Western mysticism, 115
energy, cosmic (*chi, ki, prana*), 187, 191
English medieval mystics, 21, 45
enlightenment, 118, 131; Buddhist, 10, 18, 113, 143–4, 150, 173; Christian, 144–5; and correct bodily posture, 193–4; and experience of true self, 63; and forgetfulness of self, 168; and mediation of teacher, 186; momentary, 137; and *mu*, 112; necessary for working for humanity, 172, 173, 175; and presence of God, 121–2; shocking into, 149; training for, 179
Eriugena, John Scotus, 17
erotic, the, mysticism and, 135–6, 138–9
Eve, 139
evil, 158, 175; conversion to, 151
existentialism, 79, 120
Exodus, Book of, 18, 48
Ezechiel, 145

faculties, contemplative, 179
faith, 99, 171; basis for ecumenical dialogue, 66, 68; and belief, 68–70, 76, 77, 79, 92, 92n; dark, 66, 122, 123, 133; knowledge born of religious love, 65; naked, 66–7, 69, 69n, 77, 84, 85, 122, 123; not prerogative of Christians, 69, 76–7; nourished by exterior revelation, 65–6, 68, 70; pure, 66, 84, 85; role of Christ, 67, 70
fear, liberation from, 113
feelings; acceptance of one's, 156–7, 157n, 158, 164, 184; check on (Ignatius), 158, 161; early Christians and following one's, 160–1; and 'emotional honesty', 161; in the mystical life, 159
fencing, 109, 181
fidelity, 78
Fiji fire-walkers, 190
flower arrangement, 46, 109, 187
forgiveness, 75, 131
formulations, truth and, 81–2, 82n, 83, 85
four noble truths, 113
Francis de Sales, St, 24
friendship, mystical, 141–2, 163

Gamaliel, 74, 76
Gandhi, Mahatma; debt to Gospel, 80; just anger, 178; on Mahatmaship, 171–2; and mysticism in action, 26, 28, 29; and non-violence, 80, 101, 177, 178; sacrifice of self in intercession, 170
Garrigou-Lagrange, Réginald, 29n
Genesis, Book of, 118
Gerson, Jean, 19, 20, 26
Gilson, Etienne, 21n
God; action and union with, 26; allness and nothingness, 99, 121; experience of fatherhood of, 46, 47, 49, 54, 56, 59, 76, 134; indwelling, 142; inundation by love of, 104–5; knowledge through love and unknowing, 18, 20; limitless love of, 62, 69, 70, 103–4, 136; mystery, 81, 114, 121–2, 127, 133, 185; steadfast love of, 82–3, 85;

Fount Paperbacks

Fount is one of the leading paperback publishers of religious books and below are some of its recent titles.

- ☐ SQUARE WORDS IN A ROUND WORLD Eric Kemp 95p
- ☐ THE HOLY SPIRIT Billy Graham 95p
- ☐ REACHING OUT Henri Nouwen 95p
- ☐ DEATH & AFTER: WHAT WILL REALLY HAPPEN?
  H. J. Richards £1.25
- ☐ GO AN EXTRA MILE Michael Wood 95p
- ☐ HAPPY FAMILIES Anthony Bullen 95p
- ☐ THE NEW INQUISITION? SCHILLEBEECKX AND KÜNG
  Peter Hebblethwaite £1.25
- ☐ CHRISTIANITY AND OTHER RELIGIONS
  John Hick & Brian Hebblethwaite £1.50
- ☐ TOWARDS THE DAWN Clifford Hill £1.25
- ☐ THE POPE FROM POLAND John Whale £1.50
- ☐ THE FAITH OF AN ANGLICAN Gilbert Wilson £2.95
- ☐ PRAYER FOR PILGRIMS Sheila Cassidy £1.50

All Fount paperbacks are available at your bookshop or news-agent, or they can also be ordered by post from Fount Paperbacks, Cash Sales Department, G.P.O. Box 29, Douglas, Isle of Man, British Isles. Please send purchase price, plus 10p per book. Customers outside the U.K. send purchase price, plus 12p per book. Cheque, postal or money order. No currency.

NAME (Block letters) _____

ADDRESS _____

_____

_____